PAVEL IS A GEORDIE

To Robert

Best Wishes

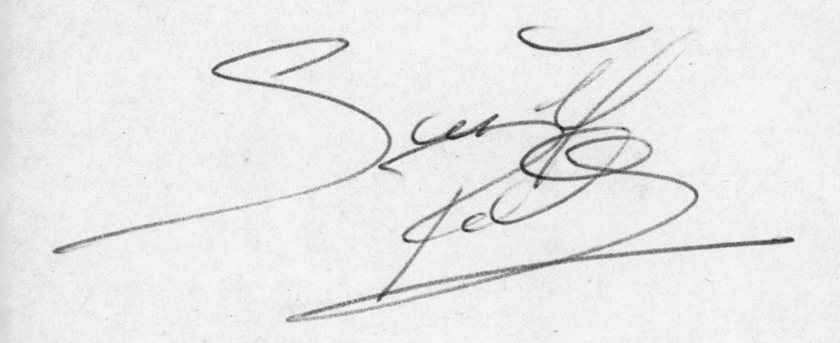

PAVEL IS A GEORDIE

Pavel Srnicek

Will Scott

Published in 2015 by Mojo Risin' Publishing

A catalogue record for this book is available from the British Library

ISBN-13: 9780993442421

Cover photography © Andy Thompson of Singe Vert Photography

Cover and plate section design
Andrew Brewster, PrintNV

Printed & bound in the UK by CPI Group (UK) Ltd

Proudly published up North by

@mojorisinbooks

THIS BOOK IS DEDICATED TO

My daughter Vendy and son Maxim, it was, is, has been, a joy watching you both grow up.

I am a proud father. My father Pavol, he hated sport, but he was the be-all and end-all.

And my mother, Bernadette, who still cooks and irons my clothes when I visit her in Bohumín.

I think I am her sweetheart.

CONTENTS

FOREWORD

Spending the first ten years of my football career away from St James' Park didn't mean I wasn't aware of what was going on at my home town club. As a Geordie and a Newcastle United supporter, I always kept a keen interest on what was happening on Tyneside in the early stages of my career at Southampton and Blackburn.

Although it was common for clubs to sign foreign players in the early 1990s, the market wasn't saturated the way it is now, but it was certainly unusual for teams to invest in foreign goalkeepers. And Pavel's arrival on Tyneside certainly caused a stir. He turned up on the club's doorstep when it was struggling at the wrong end of the old Second Division. It must have been a baptism of fire for the young Czech goalkeeper. Not only did he have to adapt to a new style of football he had to settle in to a new town and culture. As a consequence, like the team, he struggled.

I heard all about the 'dodgy keeper' chants from a mischievous United faithful on my frequent visits home and wondered how he'd cope with that. To Pav's credit he knuckled down; won over those sceptical fans; established himself as a top Premier League goalkeeper and the 'dodgy keeper' chants became nothing but a footnote in history.

Mind you I still loved playing against him! I always scored past Pav at both St James' Park and Ewood Park when I lined up against the team I supported as a boy. I netted just about every time he was in goal. And once I became a Newcastle player in

1996, I still enjoyed smashing the ball past him in training. It was nothing personal I liked scoring against anyone and everyone.

Pav's time at St James' Park was never easy and he saw off several challenges from some very good goalkeepers before winning the coveted number one jersey. He also clashed with managers Kevin Keegan and Kenny Dalglish over his claim to the goalkeeper's crown and eventually left because of it. I know it almost broke his heart to leave because he'd come to love Newcastle in the same way only a Geordie can love the city and the club. But in all my time on Tyneside, Pav is one of the most honest professionals I have met in my career. He is one of football's good guys; was a great servant to Newcastle United; always gave 100 per cent; tried his best and that is why he was adopted as a Geordie by the club's fanatical following.

It's incredible to think he came from a small village in the Czech Republic to appear on the world stage as an international footballer. The odds of that happening are astronomical. And that is what makes Pavel's story such an interesting read. With more than a few tales from the Entertainers' era. *Pavel is a Geordie*, is not only a must-have book for every Newcastle United fan but for football fans all over the world.

Alan Shearer

CHAPTER 1
PAVEL'S RETURN

I wouldn't swap a World Cup, Champions League or Premier League winner's medal for that reception. The cocktail of euphoria, adrenaline and fear was coursing through every vein of my anatomy as I ran towards the Gallowgate End. Even now it still feels like a surreal, out of body experience.

I'd experienced everything in my life and career until that moment, or so I thought. And it happened so quickly. In less than a moment: Shay Given signalled to the bench to come off because he was injured, and Glenn Roeder, the manager, turned to me and said, 'You're going on.' I didn't have time to think, prepare or get warmed up. Before I knew it, I was out of my tracksuit, standing on the sidelines and being thrown in to the proverbial gladiators' arena, in a swirling cauldron of sound. More than 50,000 spectators' chants segued from 'One Shay Given' into 'Pavel is a Geordie', and I'm running towards the Gallowgate to take a goal kick. The noise was deafening and building up to a crescendo. I wasn't sure I could handle the situation. I was shaking. The hairs on the back of my neck were standing to attention and my heart was racing. There were only three minutes left. We were leading 3-1 against Tottenham, thanks to first half goals from Keiron Dyer, Obafemi Martins and skipper Scott Parker. I tried to compose myself, but I was struggling. Then I ran up to take the goal kick... and made a right arse of it. The ball bobbled about 50 yards along the ground.

After the match I delayed going back into the changing room and stayed out on the pitch longer than any of the other players. I wanted to eat, drink, and ingest every last drop of the exhilarating atmosphere. It was a fantastic memory, one that will stay with me for the rest of my life. It was like I could still hear the crowd and I wanted to prolong that feeling. I felt like I could burst at any second.

When I got into the dressing room everyone was congratulating me, patting me on the back and shaking my hand. Once the good wishes were over the lads started taking the piss about the goal kick I'd made a complete arse of. But the response from my team mates was incredible. Everybody was happy for me because they knew what it meant. The emotion from them was genuine. I could see it in their eyes. They also made it known they were surprised at the reception I received and confessed they'd never witnessed anything like it. Some of the lads even likened it to Alan Shearer's testimonial, which was extraordinary, I have to admit. Shearer is a legend and a god in Newcastle, so to be put alongside such a Geordie icon was flattering. I was humbled.

I know I shouldn't have been surprised. But when you consider I first arrived on Tyneside in 1991, and this game was 15 years later, I just couldn't comprehend it. Nearly a generation of supporters had passed through the turnstiles since I last played at Newcastle. Some fans would've died, got older and maybe stopped going for one reason or another. Then there were the younger element that would not have seen me play. The applause and appreciation can only be likened to the ovation I received when I made the save of my life against Everton back in 1995. The one Gordon Banks rated in his top ten saves of all time. I never expected that to be beaten, never mind topped. But it was against Tottenham.

Football hasn't made me a rich man in monetary terms but the memories of my time at St James' Park have made me the wealthiest man in the world. I went to my friend Lorenzo Terrinoni's house and met up with my other good mates Denis Martin and Tom Sweeney. We were all still buzzing after the game. Denis and Tom had been to the match and were full of how everyone was talking about it in the pubs in town. Lorenzo was working in his restaurant and told me that everyone who came in was talking about my dream return. I remember pinching myself and wondering whether it was all an hallucination. It was an unbelievable feeling. I thought, I would love to stay here forever; to coach or something like that. To give something back to those who have stood by and supported me. But no sooner was I thinking and planning this than a few months later the dream comes to an end, courtesy of the arrogant Sam Allardyce.

Ironically, I started in goal against Allardyce's Bolton at the Reebok on Boxing Day, three days after the Spurs game, while my first appearance on the bench for United was when Wanderers visitedSt James' Park, in October. They won 2-1. Shay Given and Steve Harper were still injured, so Tim Krul made the trip to Bolton with the team and warmed the bench. Shay and Steve weren't the only big names missing. There were several experienced personalities absent from the squad that travelled to the North West. Consequently, Glenn Roeder put out arguably the club's youngest ever back four in a line up. Teenagers Paul Huntington and David Edgar were the full backs, while 20-year-old Steven Taylor and Peter Ramage, 23, partnered each other at the heart of the defence.

We started well and Kieron Dyer put us 1-0 ahead early in the game before Ramage headed an own goal past me, courtesy of a push in the back from future Magpies' favourite and captain, Kevin Nolan. It was undoubtedly a foul but for whatever reason the referee allowed the goal to stand. Nicolas Anelka got the winner from a trade mark Trotters' set-piece. A long throw was flicked on by Kevin Davies and the ball was turned back for the France striker to net from close range. It was disappointing to lose a match we should have taken something from.

It was to be the last time I played in goal for my beloved club because Shay and Steve returned to share goalkeeping duties after that. Admittedly, my best playing days were behind me, but I was content to settle for a place on the bench and help set up coaching sessions for the lads.

I started working with the academy kids, as well as being involved with the first team. I met Tim Krul and Fraser Forster and they trained with Shay, Steve and I. I was sad when Fraser eventually left because I felt the club should have kept him. I would love to have two precociously talented goalkeepers at Sparta Prague, like Tim and Fraser. The club should have kept them out on loan until they were ready to challenge and push each other, unless they could get big money for them. United only got £2m for Fraser yet he went to

Southampton for £10m. Newcastle could have banked that money.

It has been a privilege to have played football in the Czech Republic, England, Portugal and Italy. When I am coaching the goalkeepers at Sparta Prague, I like to mix it up, so one day I'll do an Italian session, another day it will be a Portuguese session and so on. It prevents them becoming bored and ensures enthusiasm levels are soaring. If I only did the English training sessions, they wouldn't like it because the levels of fitness were phenomenally high and hard. There wasn't much in the way of technique in England, just bang! bang! bang! The way I coach makes it a bit more interesting for the goalkeepers because I offer a bit more variety, using both the European and British way and mixing it up.

Shay didn't like the European sessions I put on. He liked his bang, bang, bang, routine, working like a Trojan. I would guess if I went back to Newcastle tomorrow, it would be the same sessions from when I first played at Benwell in 1991. Maybe that's a trifle harsh. The sessions have changed a little but there's hardly any work done on the angles, positioning or technique. That is the English way.

I was living in Italy when I got a call from Steve Harper in late September of 2006. It's fair to say my football career was winding down around this time and I was playing for a small Italian side called Carpenedolo in the fourth tier of Italian football, on a non-contract basis. Carpenedolo is a small town in the province of Brescia. A friend of mine knew the chairman. He asked whether I would be interested in coaching the goalkeepers and keeping fit while I looked for a club.

I was living alone in a camping hotel while I rented out my house in Italy, because my family were back in the Czech Republic. I had one offer from Red Star Belgrade but it was immediately withdrawn when they found out I was 38. I went back home to see my family in Ostrava around this time, and spoke with my wife about the next step forward in our lives. We both agreed that I would go back to Italy for two weeks, and if nothing turned up then I would retire. It was an extremely difficult and emotional time for me because I was finally calling time on my career as a professional footballer. I was admitting to myself that I was finished, putting myself out to pasture. You can imagine this was quite a bitter pill to swallow.

I jumped in my car and drove through the Czech Republic. I was just approaching the Austria-Italy border when I got the call from Steve Harper. I pulled the car over to accept it.

'Hi Pav, how you doing and what are you up to?'

I told him I was playing for a small club in Italy and keeping fit, just in case a club was interested in signing me.

'What if Newcastle came in for you?'

I said, 'Yeah, good one, Steve.' I thought he was taking the piss. He wasn't.

He told me Shay was injured and he was the only fit goalkeeper along with one of the youngsters, who turned out to be Tim Krul. I think maybe Steve had told the gaffer, Glenn Roeder, I was naturally fit and could resolve the goalkeeper crisis. The Newcastle boss asked whether I would be interested in coming over so he could check out my fitness. It was a no-brainer, I instantly said 'Yes, that would be fantastic!' The thought of returning to St James' Park was a dream come true. It was like all of my birthdays and Christmases had come at once. I immediately turned the car around. I was about five hours from home but, with the adrenalin coursing through my body, I reckon I did it in four.

I got a flight to Newcastle the following day and met Glenn, who said I was only there for cover and that I was going to be the third choice keeper. He added that, while I looked in good shape, he needed to see me in training before he could offer me a contract. The following day I went through the warm up routine and then ten minutes into a game, Glenn came up behind the goal and said, 'Pav, it's OK, I've seen enough. Come and see me after training and we'll sort out a contract.'

I went to see Russell Cushing to negotiate an initial three month deal. Russell had been at the club long before I was there and I have known him for a long time. But when we met in his office I said 'Russell, whatever you offer me I will take it'. It was a pleasure to be back on Tyneside and I would've played for nothing if I am honest. So he showed me some numbers and, it wasn't a fortune, but it was a fair salary for a third choice goalkeeper, knocking on a bit but not quite ready to draw his pension. Red Star Belgrade actually came back in and tried to sign me when they realised I wasn't fat, finished and ready for the glue factory. But I told them it was too late because I had signed for, what felt like, my home-town club, Newcastle. Maybe I was being sentimental but that is what it felt like. Playing and living in Newcastle gave me so much pleasure, satisfaction and a sense of belonging.

When I left Newcastle in 1998 Freddy Shepherd said if I ever wanted to come back, just give him a call. I never did. I don't know why because it's my spiritual home. I had two opportunities to return after I left. The first time was when Ruud Gullit was manager. I was told Gullit didn't rate Shay Given, and Simon Smith, United's goalkeeping coach at the time, was asked to get a message through to me to see whether I'd be interested in going back. This was when I was in my second year at Sheffield Wednesday. I never found this out until Bobby Robson was boss, a few years later. I found it hard to believe Simon wouldn't pass the message on, after all, we were friends for years.

I met Simon when he played for Gateshead in the Conference. We used to meet up to train together when I either came back for pre-season training early, stopped on at the end of the season or when the internationals were on. It got me wondering why I didn't get this message. Maybe he was worried I would take his job, which wasn't the case. I had no intention of moving into coaching at that time. I was still a young professional goalkeeper and just wanted to play. Nevertheless, there are no hard feelings and I couldn't be happier for him now he's back at St James' Park as Steve McClaren's goalkeeping coach.

The second time I had the opportunity was when I had just signed for Cosenza in 2003. Russell Cushing called to see whether if I would like to come back to the club. I was gutted. If only he had rang a week earlier. I told him I would love to return, but I was under contract I couldn't get out of it. Typical!

Glenn was a great guy. Initially, I was only supposed to stay at the club for three months. But the gaffer approached me well before that was up and asked whether I would like to stay until the end of the season, which I was more than happy to do. I was delighted to be back at the club. In my first game for the reserves, I kept a clean sheet, in a goalless draw against Wigan at Kingston Park, where a teenage Andy Carroll also played. Everything was working out just fine.

I generally kept myself to myself and tried not to get involved in club politics, although it was a difficult year for the boss. One problem I encountered was the number of cliques, particularly with the foreign players. They all seemed to stick together in a group. There didn't seem to be the bond, camaraderie and unity we had back in the 90s. Albert Luque, Emre and Obafemi Martins all spoke Italian or Spanish together and rarely any English. Luckily for me I spoke both Italian and English so I could understand what they were saying. The English players were all asking me what was being said. I tried to act as a buffer rather than becoming embroiled in any personal politics. The British lads were forever telling them, rather aggressively at times, to speak English. It wasn't good for morale and I think it made the English players suspicious that the foreign lot were talking about them. We never had this problem in my time because all of the foreigners mixed, got on with the British lads and spoke English.

Glenn was unlucky at Newcastle. He did a great job at steadying the ship, which had been run aground by the previous incumbent, Graeme Souness, the season before. And he was mainly left with the expensive misfits Souness had brought in. Furthermore, Roeder was always going to be up against it with two factions in the camp pulling in different directions. You could feel he was losing the respect of the dressing room as the season went on because he was a nice guy. He never really put his foot down and I don't think it was in Glenn's nature to be a disciplinarian. I think the players sensed it and took advantage. When that happens the players don't put themselves out for the coach. I felt this was the same when John Carver took over as caretaker manager from Alan Pardew. It was a real shame because Roeder's intentions were honest and he had been a great captain for the club when he was a player.

The results were poor until mid-November. There was a mass demonstration after we lost 1-0 at home to relegation favourites Sheffield United and dropped into the bottom three. Thousands of supporters had gathered outside the entrance of the Milburn Stand voicing their displeasure at the chairman, Freddy Shepherd.

Newcastle supporters didn't really appreciate the Magpies' chairman, but I always got on with Freddy Shepherd. I could see it from both sides – when you know how passionate the Geordies are about their football and how much they live and breathe it, you can understand their feelings and their want for someone to blame and shout at. I remember after one game Freddy said, 'Can you do me a favour, Pav?' I'm thinking, he's the chairman, why is he asking? I am his employee. He can order me to do anything. He owns half the club. Then he says, 'It's my mother's birthday. Can you take these flowers up to her in the lounge?' I was his mother's favourite player. He added, 'She would probably like your shirt as well.' I thought no problem. I gave her the shirt and signed my gloves. I've never seen her so happy as when I presented them to her. She gave me a hug and a kiss and said, 'You stay with me, Pav.' She turned to Freddy and said, 'Son, this is the best player at the club. You'd better give him a good contract.' I'm thinking, Freddy, you should listen to your mam. This was my boss and she was talking to Freddy like he was a little boy. It was very funny.

Freddy's mother always came to see me when we played. I was very sad to hear she had died. I didn't find out until a few months after her death. It was when I was at Portsmouth. Had someone told me I would have gone to the funeral because she was a lovely woman.

I remember around this time Shay was interviewed in the press and he was quoted as saying the club needed some heavy investment in players if it was to move forward. A message was quickly returned to Shay from Freddy. The chairman made it quite clear it wasn't the goalkeeper's place to comment on club business and that he should concentrate on his own performance. There was a little bit of tension between the United chief and the club's number one but it was soon forgotten.

We rode the storm and managed to put a good run of results together, losing only once in the eight games after the Sheffield match, lifting us out of the drop zone and up to 11th. We got as high as ninth but then results and performances dropped below par and there was more unrest. I suppose it didn't help Glenn that he couldn't call upon Michael Owen. Owen was the country's top striker but had injured himself in the 2006 World Cup the previous summer. His goals could have had Newcastle challenging for a UEFA Cup qualifying place.

The memory of Michael Owen playing football for Newcastle does not resonate at all. I remember Michael Owen for one thing and one thing only... horse racing. That's all he was interested in. He was injured all season. He used to come in every morning with his racing newspaper and talk about horses, betting and how you win money. I can't remember a conversation involving football. I recall one occasion when he flew into training in his helicopter. It was astounding. It didn't seem right for a player to come to training in a helicopter. It was more suited to a film set in Hollywood. His pilot just sat in the seat and watched the session. After Owen had finished training he flew him away somewhere else. I sat next to Owen in the dressing room one time. I felt like he was Bill Gates and I was someone trying to buy a computer from him. That was the difference in wealth, I felt.

We went out of the League Cup in the fifth round at Chelsea, and got thumped 5-1 at home in the FA Cup to Championship outfit Birmingham. It was an embarrassing defeat. We fared better in the UEFA Cup. We qualified through the Intertoto Cup, and because we were the last team in the competition, the rules dictated we won the trophy. This kind of gets overlooked. I know it wasn't the FA Cup or League Cup but it was an achievement of sorts. As for the UEFA Cup itself, we went out in the last 16 to Louis van Gaal's AZ Alkmaar on away goals. We won the first leg at home 4-2 but lost the return 2-0 in the AFAS Stadion. It was a great shame because we played really well at home. But for some sloppy defending we would've been in the quarter-finals of the competition.

The season more or less ended for Newcastle following a 2-1 home victory over Liverpool in February. I say ended because we only won one more league game after that, at Sheffield United. It was a great match played in appalling conditions. I thought at one stage the fixture was going to be postponed because of the rain and surface water on the pitch. The supporters on both sides generated a fantastic atmosphere and the contest ebbed and flowed. I think we just about edged it and deserved our 2-1 victory. Nobby Solano and Obafemi Martins netted for us, while former United bad boy Craig Bellamy opened the scoring for the Reds.

The season couldn't end quickly enough for our fanatical supporters following the slump in fortunes through March and April. I remember the penultimate game of the season at home to andBlackburn. It was a pitiful surrender by the team and a 2-0 loss. The writing was on the wall for Glenn after that fixture, although you can't blame the manager for the team's performance. Most of the players came back onto the pitch to show their appreciation for the support they'd received during the season, although there were a couple who didn't come back on, namely Stephen Carr and Titus Bramble. Glenn tried to fight fires after the game but the following day he resigned, or was pushed. Nigel Pearson took charge for the club's last game of the season which was drawn 1-1 at Watford. A week after that Sam Allardyce was installed as the Newcastle manager.

I asked to see Sam soon after he got the job but we never had a proper meeting. He was coming out of the entrance door at the training ground, at Benton, when I asked if I could have a word with him about his plans. Sam more or less dismissed me saying, 'I'm not going to offer you a new contract because you're too old.' It was conversation which lasted no more than two minutes, and he spent most of it looking at his fingers. You could see he was in a hurry and wanted to get away from me. There was a total lack of respect on his part.

Allardyce had a similar arrogant attitude to Kenny Dalglish. One of the club's secretaries at the time told me, 'Pav, he [Allardyce] is the nastiest man I have ever met.' People reading this may think I am being myopic or have a polarised opinion of people. But I wasn't the only one to get this feeling from the likes of Dalglish and Allardyce. Steve Harper rang me when he heard the news and said he would've bet his house I'd have been kept on had Glenn stayed. It has been the story of my life to be honest. Right place, wrong time, or vice versa.

I couldn't help thinking, what if Alan Shearer hadn't wanted to take a year off from football when he retired, and moved alongside Glenn when he stopped playing? I know I'm talking hypothetically but could you imagine how well the club would've done under Alan with Freddy Shepherd's backing?

I knew Newcastle were going to be the last club I played for and I didn't want it any other way. People say it is best to go out on a high and I did. I know in reality I began my career in the Czech Republic, but I felt my football career was metaphorically born in Newcastle and finished 15 years later in Newcastle. It was a fitting fairytale end.

I finally got to say goodbye to all of those people who stood by me through the trials and tribulations of my career at St James' Park. I never had a chance to say goodbye before. Ironically, it was probably the happiest year of my life. There was no stress, a fantastic club, supporters loved me and I was doing a job I loved for the club I have loved all of my life. Yet there was a sad aspect to my return to Newcastle.

Everything may have been going well for me on the pitch but I couldn't say this was the case off it. My wife never moved back with me to Tyneside. She stayed at home in Ostrava, and when I returned to the Czech Republic after my year in England we got divorced. So on the one hand Newcastle gave me my life but on the other I suppose it took a large part of it away as well.

CHAPTER 2
KENNY CONFLICT

Terry Gennoe approached me and said, 'Kenny told me to tell you you're not on the bench. Shaka is going to be on the bench today.' I could feel the blood rising within my body. I thought I was going to erupt. It felt like someone had just ripped my insides out. I couldn't believe it. I punched the wall as tears of anger started trickling down my face.

'Terry, I'm going to fucking kill him! Tell him I'm going to fucking kill him!' I ran down to the hotel reception area, where we were staying in Manchester prior to our FA Cup semi-final against Sheffield United, and waited for the bastard. My temper was rising by the second. And then I saw him walking down the stairs, not a care in the world, and the red mist took hold of me. I lost all control as he ambled along, oblivious to what he'd done and to how I felt.

'You fucking bastard! I'm going to kill you!'

A woman nearby, one of the hotel staff, dropped a tray she was carrying because of the sheer volume of rage in my voice. Maybe she thought I was shouting at her. I ran to lock the entrance/exit door to the reception, so he couldn't get away. Terry, our goalkeeping coach, chased after me and gripped me in a bear hug. I managed to free one arm and took a swing at Dalglish as he tried to get past, but I missed him. The coward managed to sneak under my arm and scurried onto the coach like a little rat without saying a word. It was the fastest I'd ever seen him move. Terry released his grip and I scampered after him towards the bus and tried to get on. But, just as I got there, Dalglish told the driver to shut the door and go. I slammed my fist into window as it pulled away for Old Trafford and the game. He didn't even have the balls to look me in the eye and I was left in the hotel fuming! I was furious; I could've ripped down the hotel with my bare hands. I'm surprised I didn't. That was typical of him though – spineless and never wanting to resolve any of the shit he caused. It was just brick walls and silence; causing conflict and then avoiding the fallout from it.

While I was reflecting about what had just happened I turned around and saw Temuri Ketsbaia, oblivious to the fracas, nonchalantly walking down the stairs. He said, 'Pav, what's happening, man? Where's the bus?' They left him behind as well.

'That bastard shit himself and ran away onto the bus!'

The Georgian was a bit confused and couldn't really comprehend what was going on.

'Yeah, OK, what about me?' He had to take a taxi to Old Trafford.

After I composed myself I rang a good friend of mine, Denis Martin, from Durham and told him what had happened. I was still infuriated and emotional, trying to comprehend what had just happened. Denis just said, 'Wait there, I'll come and get you.' I sat in my room and watched the game, which we won 1-0, thanks to an Alan Shearer strike. And, by the time it had finished, Denis was there to take me home.

The reason I exploded was because it was my turn to sit on the bench, yet Dalglish chose Shaka. Shaka and I were both in the last year of our contracts and after months of ignoring me – being excluded from the first team squad, training on my own - an arrangement was put in place where Shaka and I would share bench duties in alternative games. Why was the arrangement agreed? I'm not completely sure. Maybe the United hierarchy had told Kenny he had to start including me in his match day squad. It was out of the blue because I had trained on my own for months.

Dalglish did not give a reason or excuse as to why he went back on the agreement. I would say he went back on his word, but Dalglish's word isn't worth shit. He just made the decision and sent one of his minions to tell me. He probably knew I would kick off if he told me to my face. That is why he sent Terry to tell me. Dalglish treated me like a piece of shit in all my time with him at Newcastle and I'd had enough.

When I got back to the club, on Monday morning, I went to see Freddie Fletcher. In hindsight that was a mistake because he was Dalglish's good mate. I told him straight: 'I can't bear to be around him at the club or at the training ground because he treats me like a piece of shit, and you know he does, so I'm going home for a couple of weeks to clear my head.' Freddie disagreed with what I had told him and reckoned the fault clearly lay at my door. Fletcher added that I have had problems with every manager at United and should look at myself rather than blame others. His response shocked me. Admittedly, I wasn't happy when I wasn't playing under Keegan. No player is happy when they're out of the side. But it was never like this. Kevin respected me and never treat me like shit, unlike Dalglish. Furthermore, I never had any problems with Jim Smith or Ossie Ardiles.

I bumped into Terry Mac in the corridor after this meeting and told him I had to get away otherwise I would kill Dalglish. His reply astounded me: 'You think you're the only one capable of doing that? Do you not think Kenny knows people who could kill you?' I thought that was a bit of an odd thing to reply with, but I dismissed the idle threat and laughed. I would've killed him had I got the chance. Freddie and Terry were both protecting Dalglish. But had they gone around the dressing room and asked whether the other players favoured Kenny, they would've been in for a big surprise. The feeling of antipathy towards the former Liverpool manager wasn't exclusively mine. Nevertheless, I went back to the Czech Republic to clear my head and returned to Newcastle after a week. Nothing was said when I returned and I continued to train on my own. Surprisingly, when I got back, I was on the bench for the next game, a trip to Arsenal. As luck would have it, my last taste of life in the dugout came two weeks later at the venue of our FA Cup semi-final, Old Trafford. It's ironic how football does that to you.

The reason for my discontent with Dalglish, or the catalyst for our estrangement, came just after the pre-season tour of Ireland and the Umbro Tournament at Everton. He got the three goalkeepers, Shay, Shaka and I, together prior to pre-season training and told us that we were all very good goalkeepers and he wasn't sure which one of us would start the season as the club's number one. We went to Ireland to play in a tournament, against PSV Eindhoven and Derry City. I played in the match against Derry where we won 2-0. I remember the trip to Ireland well, because Shay was very popular there. We also played in a mini tournament at Everton. I played against Ajax, where we lost 3-0.

It was no surprise when another goalkeeper, in the shape of Shay Given, arrived at St James' Park that summer. I had seen it all before. A new shot stopper turned up on Tyneside before the beginning of every season. I'd become accustomed to it. I was still confident in my own abilities and I would eventually earn the right to wear the number one shirt. I was aware of Shay Given before he turned up on our doorstop. I remember the previous season when he helped Sunderland to win the First Division title. He kept 16 clean sheets in 17 appearances for the club, so you tend to notice statistics like that from other goalkeepers at other clubs.

Once pre-season training and the friendly games were over, I said to Shaka and Shay that we should go and see the gaffer to clear up who will start and where we stand. Kenny shocked us at first because he wanted Shaka and I to share our Champions League bonus from the previous season with Shay. Shaka made it known he was fine with that as long as we all share the bonus and appearance money for the forthcoming campaign. Up to that point, the way Kenny was talking, it looked as if the three of us were going to be rotated; one in goal, one on the bench and one in the stands. When we tried to clear up that conundrum, Kenny said no, the third choice will not be getting a share of the bonuses. I countered that by telling him, in that case, it wasn't fair Shay should get a share of our Champions League bonus from the previous campaign, which was £20,000 each.

It really pissed me off when Kenny asked us to share our Champions League bonus. I worked really hard for it. Shaka and I had nothing against Shay, in fact, you could tell he was uncomfortable and embarrassed by the talk. He was squirming in his chair while we were discussing it. Dalglish immediately responded by saying, 'Pav, you're third choice goalkeeper.' Consequently, I came into training the day after this meeting and found I had to train alone, while Shay and Shaka trained together or with the first team. Ten minutes before we finished training, Terry Gennoe would come over and work with me, because he felt sorry for me.

You could feel a wind of change around this time. The feel good factor we previously had encountered under Kevin was slowly evaporating. Throughout the summer and pre-season, we had been constantly linked with new arrivals, while speculation raged about who was about to leave Tyneside; none more so than Les Ferdinand.

Despite the constant conjecture it was still a shock when Les left. Why did he leave? Maybe he had the same feelings about Dalglish as I did. Maybe he was told he wasn't going to play as often, or the board were saying he had to be sold to balance the books; I don't know. I have never spoken to Les about why he left or what the reasons were behind it. Les was one of the nicest men I have ever met in football. He wouldn't say anything disparaging about anyone but I bet he was upset at having to leave.

As bad luck would have it, the day after Les agreed to sign for Tottenham, Alan Shearer got injured at Goodison Park in our pre-season tournament. The club contacted Les and asked if he would remain at St James' Park. Even Alan called to see if he could persuade his strike partner to stay on Tyneside. Despite wanting him to remain a Newcastle player, I wasn't surprised he went ahead and signed for Spurs. Les had given his word he would put pen to paper for the club he supported as a boy. And being a man of honour you wouldn't expect him to go back on a promise.

We were down to one experienced striker in Faustino Asprilla and one untried novice in Jon Dahl Thomasson as we approached the curtain raiser against my future employers, Sheffield Wednesday. I say one experienced striker but it wasn't really because Peter Beardsley was still at the club. He was on the bench with me that day. As it happens we played well and Tino had a fantastic game, netting a brace. The same can't be said for Tomasson, who seemed to freeze on the big day. He had an early chance, which he fluffed, and he never seemed to recover from it during his time at St James' Park.

Games were coming thick and fast thanks to qualifying for the Champions League. We were unbeaten throughout August. A 2-1 triumph over Wednesday was followed by two home victories; 2-1 over Dynamo Zagreb and 1-0 against Aston Villa. Remarkably, John Beresford scored all three goals. Dalglish had pushed him forward into left midfield following the signings of Stuart Pierce and Alessandro Pistone. Bez also managed a brace against Dynamo Kiev in Russia later on in the competition. A nail-biting 2-2 draw in Zagreb, thanks to strikes from Tino and Temuri Kesbaia, saw us qualify for the league stage of the competition.

I said in the previous chapter how Newcastle's season effectively ended after a game against Liverpool. The same could be said after we beat Spanish giants Barcelona on Tyneside. Yes, I know we got to the FA Cup final but it was hardly champagne football on the way to Wembley. The atmosphere was electric at St James' Park, and Keith Gillespie and Tino had arguably their greatest games in a black and white shirt. I watched from the bench as Gillespie tortured the Barca left back while our maverick Columbian bagged a memorable hat-trick.

Defeats home and away to PSV Eindhoven; a loss in the Nou Camp; a 2-2 away draw and 2-0 home victory over Kiev weren't quite good enough to qualify for the knock out stages of the tournament. Why? Several reasons really. The manager employed negative tactics; the squad wasn't good or strong enough and on a few occasions we lined up with five full backs in the side. It was mind boggling stuff. You couldn't second guess what Dalglish was going to do.

I remember hearing when Kenny took over from Kevin; he indicated the squad only needed tinkering with. I know my use of the English language isn't perfect but I'm sure it didn't mean ripping the team apart and bringing in has-beens and never-will-be's. Unknowns came in, such as Temuri Ketsbaia, Andreas Andersson, Alessendro Pistone, Nikos Dabizas and Jon Dahl Tomasson; followed by John Barnes, Ian Rush and Stuart Pearce. I don't want to sound disrespectful to any of those players, but the veterans he brought in were way past their best. Yes they had had great careers, won loads of trophies, but that was in the past. They weren't going to take the team forward. And were any of them really better than John Beresford, Darren Peacock, Philippe Albert, Peter Beardsley, David Ginola and Les Ferdinand? In essence, these players were the backbone of our success and progress over the previous five years.

The older players had our respect because of their great careers. They had a wealth of experience, an excellent attitude and good personalities, but they were fast losing face because they weren't quick enough to keep up with the pace of the Premier League. If Kenny had brought in one older player with vast experience, then fair enough, but not three or four. You can't carry three or four older players in your team. And when you look back at their time on Tyneside, did they really make an improvement to the team?

The guys who were brought in by Kevin, and were being phased out by Kenny, all formed a bond. We all spoke about what was happening. We encouraged and supported each other while Kenny was taking a proverbial wrecking ball to the club. The team was dismantled under him, destroyed. It's hardly surprising we stuck together, when you consider we had spent the previous five years building something special at the club only for Dalglish to come in and demolish all of the good work Keegan had put in place. I know I wasn't happy with my situation under Kevin but I never hated him. He was a good man. I could see what he was trying to do, and he did respect and treat me like a man, unlike Dalglish

It has been suggested the position was too big for Dalglish, but he must have known how significant the job was at Newcastle. He should've been able to cope with the pressure. He was a great player at Liverpool, a great manager on Merseyside and, of course, won the title at Blackburn. I don't know why he was the way he was with us. Maybe he didn't like the way we, and the people of the North-East, lived our lives. I've never met anyone quite like him. He never looked into your eyes when he spoke to you; he always had an air of superiority and treated me like dirt. This just wasn't me, he did this with everyone. He definitely thought he was better than anyone else. The way he spoke and the cutting, hurtful sarcasm was uncalled for. There have been people in my life that I haven't liked or got on with but I still gave them respect. I never felt that way about Dalglish. One of the lads once said he loves his dogs more than people. Maybe he should've got a job looking after cats and dogs or ran a farm in that case.

Kenny had such a great career and knows a lot of influential people in football who will never say a bad word against him. But I'm sure there are more than a few out there who think the way I do. There were several who played with me at Newcastle. He tried to destroy me as a man. Managers make and break careers. If he didn't like Shay then I'm positive he wouldn't have had the career he went on to enjoy. If Dalglish hadn't arrived at St James' Park I would still be there. I am convinced of it. I would be there in some capacity, as a coach more than likely.

It goes without saying, the 1997-98 campaign was the worst season of my career. There were 56 games that term including Premier League, Champions League, FA Cup and League Cup. I played only once, against Blackburn in a 1-1 draw. I was on the bench a further 13 times; unlucky for me, eh? We also finished

13th in the league. That was our worst finish in a top flight campaign since we were promoted in 1993. It was mentioned that it was a tragedy when we finished sixth in our second season back in the big time. But this was a horrendous league position. We'd finished runners up in the previous two terms.

It was said Kenny would be a good appointment for the club. He would finish the job Kevin started and finally land some much craved silverware. Dalglish's style was said to be a bit more cautious and pragmatic. This would be more successful than Keegan's open football style. So out went the fluent, eloquent, one-touch football where attack became the best form of defence. In its place, Dalglish introduced a careful, ungainly and disjointed model, that wasn't a success at all, far from it. The football was just bloody awful and, not only that, we were worse for it.

Smiles around the club had changed to frowns and it reflected Dalglish's dour personality. Training wasn't enjoyable, going to games wasn't a pleasant experience and the football was dreadful. If that wasn't bad enough our chairman and director were set up in a *News of the World* sting. Freddy Shepherd and Douglas Hall were caught on camera boasting of how they'd ripped off fans, mocking Geordie women and calling Alan Shearer 'Mary Poppins'. The season was staggering from bad to worse.

It was a shock to us all when the story broke. The players all spoke about it and were astounded. Douglas was the son of Sir John Hall and a director, while Freddy Shepherd was our chairman. We were employed by them, so the story was also about us as well. We wore the shirts that were supposed to cost only five quid. Can you imagine how the parents of those kids felt having to pay out £40 every season for a new shirt? Some families had two and three kids. That's a lot of money to shell out when you don't have much money to go around. My wife was from the Czech Republic so I wasn't insulted by the comment that all women from Newcastle were 'dogs'. But some of the players did have Geordie girlfriends or wives. It was a bad PR exercise for the club and wasn't a good way to project the club. This story didn't just stay local; it went all the way around the world.

I know it has been said that Freddy and Douglas were set up as part of a sting. And I know peoples' inhibitions are lowered when they have had a drink, but you should still watch what you say in front of people. Some stories just come and go. This story didn't just last a week and then go away. It hung around for months. It hurt the fans, it hurt the club and it hurt the city of Newcastle. I'm a great believer in fate, and it came as no surprise that this all happened while Kenny was in charge of the team. There was a cloud hanging over the club from the first day he walked into St James' Park. Kenny was bad for the club in the same way Sam Allardyce was. I didn't know Allardyce, and maybe he was a good manager, but he wasn't the right man for Newcastle and the North-East. There was an arrogance about the two men. They couldn't give a fuck about anyone. Why? Maybe because they had made enough money and were already set up for life. There's no doubt the story damaged the reputation of the club. People's perceptions were starting to change about us. In a very short time we went from being the nation's second favourite team to a laughing stock.

I should probably talk about our FA Cup run, given that I spoke earlier about an upsetting experience prior to the semi final. Obviously, I was happy for our supporters. It was the first time they had been to an FA Cup final in 24 years. But the road to Wembley is just a painful memory for me. I'm guessing it is for the fans, looking back. The team never did itself justice on the day. Dalglish will probably take credit for taking the club to its first FA Cup final in decades. But when you look at who stood in our way, it is hardly surprising we got to the final. Aside from Everton in the third round, we never met another Premier League club in the competition until the final. I wasn't involved in the squad but I was there. The best I can say about the day is that our fans performed marvellously, unlike the team.

My contract ran out at the end of this turbulent campaign yet, despite a tumultuous season of club conflict and political strife, I was offered a four-year deal worth £500,000 a year. It was a fantastic contract. The biggest deal of my career and yet I wasn't the club's number one goalkeeper. It would've set me up for life. But, with a heavy heart, I turned it down. I rang Freddie Fletcher and told him it was a fantastic contract but said I wasn't going to sign it. Fletcher rang me the following day, while I was still packing, and left a message that the offer was still on the table. I ignored the voice-mail message. He also rang me two weeks later and said, 'Pav, the contract is still here, are you going to sign it?' I knew Kenny's job was under threat so I asked whether he was staying or getting sacked. Freddie said he couldn't say what was going to happen.

Two weeks into the new season and Kenny was given the boot. I am sure Freddie Fletcher knew he was going to get sacked. When Dalglish was dismissed I asked whether the offer was still open. Much to my disappointment it had been withdrawn. They subsequently signed Sunderland goalkeeper Lionel Perez as my replacement. Had Freddie said, go away for a few weeks, have a break and then come back when you have cleared your head, I would have never left the club. Nonetheless in hindsight, as long as Dalglish was in charge, I still would've refused to sign. That is how much I hated the man. He destroyed my career. I probably would've finished my career at the Newcastle, had a testimonial and stayed coaching with the first team or the academy.

I had made the heart-wrenching decision to leave the club I loved. I was half way through packing up the house and moving lock, stock and barrel back to the Czech Republic. My friend, Denis, wanted me to rethink and stay because he knew I loved Newcastle and everything about the North-East. And of course £500,000 a year was a lot of money to reject. I was still undecided. My wife was back in my home country and I thought I'd call her and see what she said. I left the decision up to her. Denis' wife also spoke with Pavla to try and talk her into staying. I called her and spoke and, after a 20 minute chat, she told me to come home.

When we finished loading up the removal truck I took one last look around the house and its surroundings and cried! I didn't like it, but to me it was the only decision I could have made.

CHAPTER 3
BUDGIE CRAP, CRAP SALAD AND CRAP IN THE BATH

My first day at Benwell, which was where we used to train, was a baptism of fire. I had never experienced anything like it. The players and manager, Jim Smith, could not have been more welcoming. And I was happy enough with how we trained and interacted with each other. But the changing rooms were another issue. Spartan isn't the word. There was one bath, and everybody went in it! There were no showers, not one. We even had showers in the Czech Republic. And my country was a Communist state, judged to be no more than a third world country by most of the western world. I looked at the water and it was rank – there was scum floating on the surface. It was dirty and it stank to high heaven. And I was the last one in after training. I was thinking oh no, I've got to get in that. I was expecting dead things to be in it – it was disgusting.

I look around, not knowing whether to get in the bath or just run for the hills, and see Budgie, John Burridge, sitting on the toilet, door wide open, having a crap and reading the newspaper. And he's having a conversation with me and the rest of the lads like it's the most natural thing in the whole world. I'm thinking what the hell is going on here? I'd never seen anything like it in my life. It is funny looking back on this time. Needless to say, I didn't get in the bath. I waited until I got back to the hotel for a nice shower. I continued that habit until we moved to Maiden Castle where they had showers.

It will probably come as a surprise to many Newcastle United supporters that I nearly joined another British team. Initially, I had a trial with Leicester City, then managed by David Pleat. He is remembered by most people for that funny jig on the pitch when he saved Luton Town from relegation in the 1980s. Ludvik Colin, a Yugoslavian agent who lived in Ostrava, approached the Banik chairman and said he knew a club who would take me for £350,000. That was big money in the Czech Republic back in 1990.

The trial went well. I was there for a week and at the end of the seven days I went to see Pleat in his office. I remember knocking on the door and he was tucking into a mince pie. Funny how these things stick in your memory. He was a messy eater, talking with his mouth full, and there was pie all over the place. In fact there was more pie on the table than he'd eaten. He said he wanted to sign me but couldn't get the cash together. He asked whether I could hang on for a month so he could raise the money. I was happy to wait so they got me to put my name to a pre-contract forbidding me to sign for anyone else during that time. The agreement was, if they couldn't raise the cash after the month had expired then I was free to find another club. In the end Leicester couldn't get the money together so the agent set me up with a trial at Newcastle.

Going out on trial was common practice in the Czech Republic at the time. There were no scouts from European clubs watching you, or at least very few, unlike now where it seems all Premier League clubs have someone somewhere looking for a new starlet.

Also, you have to remember, to get a move you had to play about 75 per cent of international games for your national team. That is why no one came to the Czech Republic to watch players. I got through because of a loophole. I have a French passport because my mother is French, so it took me a week to get my work permit to play in the UK, while it took Ludek Miklosko three months for a licence, despite him being the Czech number one goalkeeper. I was only 20 years old. I had no international experience other than three caps for the under-21s when I was 17.

A club representative met me at the airport and I lived the first few months of my life in Newcastle at the New Kent Hotel, Jesmond. The owner of the hotel was a guy called Alan. I can't remember his second name but he was a funny man; a great guy.

My first day at training saw me involved with some shooting practise and then there was a game, made up of the first team, reserves and some youth team players. At the end of my week's trial I played for the reserves at Anfield against Liverpool where we won 3-1. Peter Beardsley was in the Reds' side that night. Obviously I didn't know it was him at the time, although I did recall his face from the game. I remember he was a brilliant player but he couldn't get past me, no matter how hard he tried. It wasn't until he rejoined us from Everton a couple of seasons later that I remembered, or rather he reminded me about that game. He was very complimentary about my performance, saying I had played fantastically well that night.

After the reserve game, a Liverpool official enquired what the situation was at Newcastle and asked whether I would be interested in joining them instead. I can't remember who he was. I told him I wasn't sure what was happening but would let him know. But there was no need to get in touch with them because the following day Jim Smith offered me a contract. I don't know whether they asked me to sign because of Liverpool's interest but I was happy to put pen to paper for the Magpies nonetheless. I had a good feeling about Newcastle.

Just before I signed my first contract the club said I needed to have a medical. I wasn't looking forward to it to be honest. I hate hospitals. I was exhausted and couldn't be chewed with more fitness exercises after a week of training. So I turned up at St James' Park and went into the medical room. There was this old guy there with grey hair. I can't remember his name. He asked a few questions through my interpreter about where I was from etc. He looked into my mouth, asked me to stick my tongue out and say ahh. He then asked me to turn around, which I did. He then said, 'Right, you're a big lad. You seem OK.' And that was it! Incredible! When I was at Brescia they put me on a bike, checked my heart rate, took blood and urine samples and put me through several strenuous tests. Not here, it was sit down, turn around and pick a bale of cotton. It's hilarious when you think about it.

My first contract saw me pick up £700 a week. I also got a £20,000 signing on fee. I thought I was a rich man. My wages quadrupled and I was given a lump sum as well. It was a dream move, when you consider where I came from. But despite being happy with my salary, as my career developed at United I was always one of the lowest paid professionals at the club.

Obviously I was ignorant of all this at first but when you get to know your team-mates better, or there is a new signing and you discuss your salary, you realise you're being short changed. I was thinking, hang on a minute; my wages are terrible compared to the rest of the team.

The transfer fee for Banik was brilliant. They bought a team coach and invested the rest of it. I left the club on good terms. I enjoyed my time there and was sad in some respects to leave, although my relationship soured a little when I returned after my contract ran out at St James' Park. They never paid me any wages. They tried to justify it by saying I had made enough money at Newcastle and the other players needed the money more than I did. But the move and challenge was too good an opportunity to turn down.

My wife, Pavla and my little girl, Vendy, did not join me in Newcastle until a couple of months later and by that time I had rented a house in Darras Hall, from Eddie Halman, at 234 Middle Drive. I didn't know until later that the area was a popular place for footballers to live. At the time, of course, I couldn't speak English so I had an interpreter. The house was perfect because it was close to a school for my little girl. I recently went to see it, on a visit to Newcastle, but it had been razed to the ground and a much bigger house had been built in its place.

The club set up English lessons for us, but obviously it was easier for me at first because I was with the boys at the club most of the time. But then Pavla mastered the English language better than me because I didn't want to go to school to take the lessons when I got home from training. I was just too tired. I even told Pavla I didn't want to learn English and if she did, then, she was welcome to do it. My wife picked it up really quickly but, for me, it probably took a year to get to grips with it. You'll probably find this funny but when you talk as a foreigner, you generally use your hands to get your point across. But when it comes to talking on the telephone it's a different matter. In our first year, Pavla and I would just stare at the phone when it rang and look at each other. We were frightened to pick it up! I'd say you pick it up and she would say, no, you get it. Nine times out of ten we just let it ring. I'd probably do the same now, to be honest. I mean, how many PPI claims can one have?

It goes without saying everything was new, exciting and scary at the same time. My family and I were embracing a fresh life together in a foreign country and we weren't sure what was going to happen next. This was the case when Russell Cushing contacted me to say a couple of detectives wanted to talk to us. I had never been in trouble with the police before so I had no idea what they wanted. Maybe they thought I was part of some Cold War espionage mission smuggling currency and drugs into the country. Nevertheless, they turned up and asked several probing questions about my transfer fee, salary and signing on fee. They also asked about my passport because it was French, not Czech. I had to answer the questions through my interpreter because I couldn't speak a word of English. Throughout this series of interrogations I was wondering why they were quizzing me. They should've been asking the club. Apparently my agent, Ludvig, was also under investigation for the transfer between Banik, Newcastle and him.

I didn't know what to think to be honest. I was a young man of 21, newly arrived from a Communist country. I'm guessing everyone was suspicious of people in my position, but I thought I'd left all of that behind. I only met Ludvig a few times so I didn't really know him. It was the Banik Ostrava chairman who introduced us and said he had a club for me in England. I know they spoke with Russell Cushing and everything was above board at Newcastle. I think it was all resolved pretty quickly. I don't know what happened with regards to Ludvig, though.

I read that when Mirandinha, the Brazilian striker, signed for Newcastle, Gazza was teaching him swear words and that Wednesday was Wankday. Nothing like that happened to me. The first words I learned were chicken, rice and crab, although to be honest, I did have a little trouble with my pronunciation, as you can imagine. I spent the first few months of my time living in the New Kent Hotel, Jesmond. When I came in from training I'd ask the old lady working in the restaurant for crap and rice. She would burst out laughing and I didn't know why until the owner, Alan, would ask, 'Do you want a crap, Pav?' and he'd make a fart noise with his mouth. If I met him in the street now, it would be the first thing he would say to me. Alan was a great guy and made my life more comfortable when I arrived in Geordieland.

It was awkward for me at first. I was homesick. And obviously, when you don't know the language and you hear people talking and laughing, you think, are they laughing and talking about me? It was a horrible feeling and I was a bit paranoid. I was wondering whether I would get on with everyone, will people like me or dislike me? But unlike when I joined Banik Ostrava as a youngster, I was looking forward to coming to the UK. It was an adventure and, as it happens, everyone was great with me, so I was lucky. Lee Clark and David Roche were very good to me. Rochey was a great lad but, man, could he swear. I'd never heard anything like it before, and I've never heard anything like it since. I hope he is keeping well – he could have put Chubby Brown to shame with his swearing! Roy Aitken, Benny Kristensen, Micky Quinn and Kevin Scott all invited me around for dinner to help me settle in. I also got to know Ando, John Anderson, as well.

I couldn't drive before I came to Newcastle so I enrolled in a driving school for three weeks for a crash course, no pun intended, and passed. The first few months I was in the hotel with Gavin Peacock and Andy Hunt, so they gave me a lift to training. Sometimes Jim Smith would pick me up because he was in a hotel as well. He never had a house in Newcastle because he had a property in Portsmouth and often went down to the south coast. On the odd occasion I would try to get the bus. But when my family arrived in Newcastle I got a club car.

I remember when I was in Russell Cushing's office, at St James' Park, he pointed out my car from his window. It was a white Nissan Bluebird. It was my first car. I remember the first time I took it out. I picked up my wife and daughter and drove into town. I parked it in the car park near the Civic Centre, at the back of the City Hall and baths. There was some snow lying on the streets and roads, and as I drove in to the car park, it skidded, or so I thought. I got out after I'd parked it and looked at the car and saw the left hand rear side door had been bashed in. I'm thinking, what the hell, my new car has been damaged already and I haven't even had it a day. Then I realised I'd driven into a stone bollard but didn't see it because it was covered in snow. I was shitting myself. I thought I was in for a right bollocking.

I took the car back to the club the following day and there was a guy called Scott, who looked after the cars. My interpreter told him about the accident and he was like, 'No! You damaged the car on your first day?' From that day until the day I left, every time he saw me he would shout, 'Bad driver! *Bad driver*!'

Tommy Wright, John Burridge and I were the three goalkeepers. We weren't all best friends but we got on. Maybe that was because we all wanted to be the club's number one goalkeeper, I don't know. Just a hunch.

Budgie was mental. He watched *Match of the Day* with his gloves on and then later when he went to bed, he would put them under his pillow and sleep on them. He loved the smell of his gloves. He would often say, 'Pav, smell these gloves, don't they smell great?' He was a fantastic man to work with and an inspiration to me. He grafted really hard in training every day and he worked me especially hard with some gruelling sessions. His attitude was exemplary; such dedication and such an eccentric as well. He gave me everything as a young goalkeeper and never stopped talking about the game. When I think about it, he was as big an influence on me as anyone has been over my career. He was coming towards the end of his career when I arrived at Newcastle and I was at the beginning. I think he was about 36 then. I remember saying to him: 'I hope I look as good as you when I get to your age.' And he often said, 'You have great physique and you will look even better than me if you look after yourself.'

Admittedly, I struggled with the pace of English football when I arrived. It was one hundred miles an hour. I wasn't used to that. The pace in the Czech Republic was a lot slower. The same can be said of the supporters. The demands of the Czech fans are less than those of their British counterparts. Nothing in my country could match the fervour and passion of the Kevin Keegan era. The city lived and breathed Newcastle United at that time and they still do. Sparta Prague won the treble in 2014. Could you imagine what it would be like if Newcastle ever won the double? Sparta fills their stadium only about three or four times a season, whereas Newcastle sell out just about every home game. Admittedly, there are four clubs in Prague and the support is divided, but still, the passion isn't as strong.

After training at Benwell, the players would all go upstairs where there was a small kitchen, ran by an old guy called Ronnie who seemed to have one leg shorter than the other, and we had a cup-a-soup and sandwiches. We had the same soup and sandwiches when we switched to Maiden Castle in Durham. You can imagine if he was in a Guy Ritchie movie, he'd be called Ronnie One-Leg or something. My favourite was the tomato but the mushroom was tasty too. It was fantastic. It's all changed now, of course. There was no attention to detail with your diet back then, the way it is now. We would just about eat and drink anything we wanted. As long as you performed on a Saturday or match day you would be fine. Take Peter Beardsley: he would eat chicken, drink coke and eat sweets yet he was fantastic every week. When we went on tour to Thailand and Singapore we all went out for Chinese food, yet he wouldn't have any. He said, 'Sorry boys, but I don't eat any of this stuff.' He only ate traditional English food.

It's hard to compare the time when I first joined the club to now. Everything has changed from our dietary needs to the way we train. When we used to train at Maiden Castle, three to four thousand people used to come and watch us every day because they couldn't get a ticket for a match. Now it is all behind closed doors. It was fantastic and we had a great relationship with the fans. I used to stay behind and play with the kids who turned up to watch after our training had finished. Parents would ask, 'Pav, could I get a picture with you and my son, or daughter?' It was a small gesture but I loved it and appreciated their support. After that I would then go to the gym and go through my fitness routine and stretches before I hit the showers. I went through this schedule every day until my playing career finished.

There was a father and son from Durham who came down to watch us train every day. They were both called John Dent and we became great friends. They were interested and intrigued with goalkeeping and my routine, so I often used to stop behind and chew the fat with them. It gave me an enormous sense of fulfilment and satisfaction to think that the likes of the two Johns and the rest of the supporters were getting the same enjoyment and pleasure watching us work and train. Not that I needed any more incentive, but if anything having the fans around watching motivated me to work and train even harder.

In all that time there wasn't one bit of trouble at Maiden Castle. There was one security guard. Thousands used to come and watch us and not one incident of note happened to cause any concern or alarm. They would turn up with their flasks of tea and sandwiches and sit in their camping chairs. It was fantastic. When I returned home to the Czech Republic and told friends, family and international colleagues, they wouldn't or couldn't believe what I was telling them.

All of this changed, however, when Kenny Dalglish took over from Keegan. Dalglish said he wanted the team to train behind closed doors because he didn't want scouts or other teams getting to know our tactics. But I think there was a simpler explanation: the fans didn't like him. Some supporters did make the odd comment to us players about how we played at the time but we had to live with it. They paid our wages at the end of the day. But as long as they were respectful you would listen to what they had to say. Could you imagine that happening now? They would probably claim they couldn't do it because of health and safety issues. Back then it was special, we were all close, like a unit. The people, the city and the club were all one. Now it is fragmented, disparate and apart. We'll probably never get that back at Newcastle, which is sad.

Jim Smith quit not long after I joined the club. I think he said Newcastle was unmanageable because there was a power struggle at the time, with Sir John Hall and the Magpie Group trying to gain control of the club. I bumped into Jim several times after he left Newcastle when he was manager at Derby or Portsmouth. He was always happy to see me and, likewise, I was always glad to meet up with Jim as well. My old boss says he was happy to take credit for discovering me. I always remember when I was living at the New Kent Hotel, he turned up with a bag full of new gloves, boots and training clothes. It was the first time something like that had ever happened to me. I felt blessed.

Jim had this rough growl, sounding very much like a bulldog eating a wasp. He'd pick me up and ask, 'How's your English? Or, 'Learned any words yet, Pav?' Obviously I had no idea what he was saying, so I'm just nodding and going, 'Yes, yes'. Then later on when he'd left Newcastle he'd say 'Fucking hell, you can speak English now? You took your time.' He was a hard man type of manager but he could also laugh and take the piss as well.

When Jim quit as manager, Ossie Ardiles came in and was great with me from the start. One of the first things he told me was, 'Don't read the papers because what they write is bollocks!' Not that I could read them at the time anyway. He added if I did read and listen to what they had to say it would kill me. Ossie said life is difficult enough being a foreigner in another country without having to deal with what other people say about you in the newspapers. Of course he went through it all himself when he was a player and understood what I was going through, so I really appreciated what he was trying to do for me.

Ossie's first game in charge was at home against Bristol Rovers, which we lost 2-0. We then lost 3-0 away at Notts County. Two home games followed that: a 2-2 draw with Oxford United before the new manager recorded his first victory, a 3-2 win over Oldham. We had conceded nine goals in those four games.

I made my debut on April 17 1991, ironically against Sheffield Wednesday, a team I would later join after I left St James' Park. We won 1-0. Kevin Brock scored the winning goal when he found the top left hand corner of the goal at the Gallowgate End, in front of 18,330 supporters. If I remember rightly, the Owls had their minds on Wembley, and a League Cup final appearance against Manchester United five days later. That's what the press wrote. I remember the day before the game, Budgie came up to me after training, shook my hand and said, 'You're going to play tomorrow, good luck.' That was the measure of the man, a true gentleman and sportsman. I wasn't quite sure what was happening and didn't know if I'd been picked at that stage because I couldn't speak English very well. I knew from his body language he wasn't happy, though, and later on I realised it was because he had been dropped. Why Ossie dropped him, I don't know, maybe because he wanted a younger goalkeeper and team.

Ossie took me to one side soon after and said he rated me and thought I showed promise as a young goalkeeper. He told me to go out and enjoy my debut and the experience. I kept my place, in front of John Burridge, and remained in goal for the rest of the season. In all, I played the remaining seven games. We won one, drew four and lost two, scoring seven and conceding eight. My sole focus at the back end of that season was to establish myself and do enough to remain the first choice goalkeeper for the beginning of the new campaign.

Football in England compared to the Czech Republic was worlds apart. In England the teams interacted with the goalkeepers more, as in passing back to the keeper, whereas in the Czech Republic a player would just kick the ball away. Not only that, the speed: the game was faster; it was more physical and it was more intense. I had to get used to playing in front of a full house. There was only a few thousand who came to watch us in Prague. It was tough and I struggled to get to grips with the hustle and bustle. I admit it was the first time I doubted myself as a goalkeeper. I got a few knocks, missed a few crosses and fans were calling me a dodgy keeper! These things could stay with you for the rest of your life. But I had two choices: quit and go home, or stay, fight, prove my worth and the critics wrong. I chose the latter. I was determined to show those people, pundits and supporters they were wrong. Fortunately, most supporters changed their opinion of me.

CHAPTER 4
DODGY KEEPER AND KEVIN WHO?

'Kevin who?'

'Kevin Keegan. You've never heard of him?'

'No, I don't think so.'

My interpreter went on to reel off a list of his achievements: two European Footballer of the Year awards; European Cup; UEFA Cups; FA Cup; titles in England and Germany and a former England captain. To be honest, it wouldn't have mattered whether he'd won a Nobel Prize, an Oscar or a Blue Peter badge. I still didn't know who he was.

Kevin Scott and Benny Kristensen were always helpful when new things were happening at the club. But, despite my naivety and ignorance, even they thought I was joking when I said I didn't know Kevin and Terry McDermott. But it was true. Fair enough, they had won lots of trophies and Kevin was European Footballer of the Year, twice, but I decided I would give them the same respect I held for my team-mates. That was until they both started bragging about all the trophies they had won, and we would groan, 'Not again.'

It didn't take me long to get know Kevin and understand what he was about. He changed my life and the lives of those at the club, forever. In my career, I have never come across anyone quite like Kevin Keegan. The way he talked and the ability he had to motivate players. He had such an enigmatic personality and was an extremely inspirational character. Yet his team talks were very brief. There were never any long

Churchillian *we will fight them on the beaches* monologues with him. Instead, he would come in to the dressing room before a game and would talk to us for a couple of minutes. He'd name the team and say something like, 'this is the team you're playing today. Show me you're better than them.' Then he would walk out of the dressing room. After the game he would return and say, 'Thanks lads, I would swap any of you for anyone in the world,' or words to that effect. In the five years he was boss at Newcastle it was always the same.

At Maiden Castle, where we used to train, he would stop and chat and sign autographs with fans. He was always the last one to leave the training field. He would stay until every supporter had gone or until every fan had got his signature. He certainly had charisma, charm and apparently he was a canny chanter, although I never heard him sing... apart from watching the video for *This Time*, England's World Cup single from 1982 where he was the only one who knew the words to the song and was enthusiastic about it. When he was talking on the television he was always comfortable, spoke articulately and came across well. I know he lost it on TV, that time after we beat Leeds 1-0 at Elland Road, but that was a bit different. He was under intense pressure and felt strongly about what Sir Alex Ferguson had said about whether Leeds would raise their game against us in the same way they did with Manchester United. Everything about him and his actions spoke volumes about his passion and commitment.

I remember looking forward to returning to Newcastle for the 1991-92 campaign after the end of season break. I had finished the campaign as the club's number one goalkeeper and I was keen to cement that place and improve as a keeper. But I wasn't prepared for my first pre-season training. It nearly killed me. It was all running. I couldn't get my head around it. I was thinking, I am a goalkeeper, I shouldn't be doing all this running and sprinting. We never did any of that in the Czech Republic. Certainly the goalkeepers didn't do all the running.

The worst thing about training was that I had to work out with Tommy Wright! He was a long distance running champion when he lived in Northern Ireland. He used to lap the other players in the squad, so you can imagine what he did to me. I was told to try and keep up with him. I thought, you're joking; the other players can't even keep up with him! I can't handle this. I can't go running and try to catch a ball at the same time. I could do one or the other but not both. You would think with Ossie being such a wonderfully talented footballer in his day, we would do more with the ball, but it was often left to the coaches, like Tony Galvin. But back then we did two sessions a day: one running in the morning and then one with the ball in the afternoon. I was too knackered to do the second session.

The first pre-season was the worst. There was one session where we were told to do two circuits and I didn't really understand the instruction to be honest, so I ran the first one crazy fast. Then I had nothing left in the tank for the second one because I didn't realise we were doing two. I began to enjoy training later on but I have to say I hated the first couple of seasons.

I started the new term as Ossie's number one and played in the first 15 league and cup games before I injured my knee ligaments in training. It was an unfortunate injury because it shouldn't have happened. Gavin Peacock, who signed for Newcastle from Bournemouth around the same time as me and was stopping in the same hotel, had the last effort of the training session. He shouted, 'Pav, last shot!' As he shouted, I slipped and twisted my knee. I was in plaster for six weeks after the accident. I was gutted. We had just beaten Leicester 2-0 at home, Andy Hunt and Lee Clark both scored and it was my first clean sheet of the season.

Up to then we were struggling in the league. We'd won only two games, drew four, lost nine and were lying third from bottom in the relegation zone. The Newcastle fans were giving me grief at this point, with the 'dodgy keeper' chants. Admittedly, I wasn't playing very well but I was still coming to terms with the hustle and bustle of British football. I was determined to win over not only the supporters, but some of our players who I felt didn't rate me either. I saw the older, more experienced players who knocked around together, like Liam O'Brien, Mark McGhee and Micky Quinn, and I didn't fit in when they were having a laugh. I was the only foreigner at the club and I didn't get the British sense of humour.

I always got the feeling Liam O'Brien hated me. Why? I think because I took Tommy Wright's place in the first team and he was his good friend. Then there were times when he was nasty to me, shouting and screaming at me in training, 'Fucking hell, Pav!' There was this one time when he screamed at me and I replied because I understood what he'd said, unlike previously. This shocked everyone. Our relationship did get better after I stood up to him, but prior to that we didn't have a relationship. Unfortunately, I got injured so I couldn't do anything about winning over the doubters.

This was the season United played their youngest ever side, if you remember. I was out injured, but there was an average age of 22 when we went to visit Blackburn at Ewood Park, on November 23 that year. The kids played well, as it happens, and were rewarded with a 0-0 draw against a team that was eventually promoted, and managed by Kenny Dalglish. Although not all of the youngsters who played that season went on to have a future at St James' Park, most of them went on and carved out a career for themselves: Kevin Scott, Alan Thompson, Lee Makel, Alan Neilson, David Roche, Robbie Elliott, Steve Watson and of course Lee Clark.

But talk about a rollercoaster of a season! In that term we played in a Zenith Data Systems Cup tie at Tranmere where we drew 6-6 and lost on penalties. It was a crazy game and a crazy campaign. There was a lot of pressure on Ossie at the time. He didn't have any money to buy players and he was playing all the kids. And as everyone knows, kids need time to mature and develop. Our Argentine boss didn't get as much time as he would have liked.

I had a feeling Ossie would be sacked. His English wasn't good and I felt he couldn't encourage or influence the team very well because of this. A lot of the players were laughing at his broken English and I thought several players had a lack of respect for him. It is sad for me to say because I was in a similar position being a foreigner. On the other hand, it was very difficult to understand what he was saying. So I believe his lack of communication and motivation skills were his downfall and, ultimately, cost him his job.

Ossie got sacked and Kevin Keegan came in as his replacement. And I was on to my third manager in a year. I was still recovering from my knee ligament injury when Kevin arrived and only played one more game that season: a 3-2 home defeat to Tranmere. Tommy Wright was back between the posts for the next game, a trip to Ipswich, which we also lost 3-2, and remained there for the rest of the season. Kevin preferred Tommy to me at that time. Obviously, I didn't quite get what all the fuss was about when he arrived as the new manager. But I soon got caught up in it all and what he meant to the supporters. I couldn't put my finger on it at the time but I did have a feeling something special was about to happen. Kevin had an aura and power about him. The club was skint yet he got £20m to buy new players. No one else before him could get it. I was thinking, how is that possible? He must have some charisma to talk the chairman, Sir John Hall, into investing that money in the club.

He got all of the players together when he first arrived and introduced himself and Terry Mac to us. My English still wasn't great at this point so I didn't understand a lot of what was being said. As I say, I hadn't heard the man's name before then but the Newcastle supporters loved him because he'd helped to get the team promoted ten years earlier as a player. To me, he was just another manager. And just because he was a famous player, it doesn't mean he would be a great manager. Just like we all had to prove we could play, in my eyes he had to prove he could manage. And that's how mutual respect would evolve.

When Kevin first joined us, after Ossie left, he gave us a lot of freedom. I am amazed, when I look back at the time, how we trained and how we prepared for the games compared to now. Back then we did shooting practise followed by games of five, six or seven-a-side. That's all. And we did this every single day. Some days he would say, 'Right, we're going to pick four teams, with four goalkeepers, and we're going to play a mini-tournament.' But everybody loved and enjoyed it. There was little work on tactics. It would be come in, warm up, shooting sessions and then a game.

Kevin never spent much time with me when he first arrived. I think it was because I didn't speak much English. He did have a chat when I'd returned to fitness from injury. I didn't understand much of it, mind, but I think it was about giving both Tommy Wright and I a chance to prove ourselves. Later on I got the feeling he preferred Tommy. It might have been because I wasn't very good at communicating with the players because of my English. On the other hand, I thought maybe he would be a bit more understanding because he had lived and played abroad in Germany. Not only that but when Kevin arrived I had been in the country a year, six months of which I was injured.

If life was tough on the pitch, it was even harder off it because we got burgled inside our first year on Tyneside. Thieves got into our house one evening when I was playing a game for Newcastle, which didn't help. I had a friend stopping over from the Czech Republic. I had just bought a brand spanking new, all singing and dancing television and video and had set the tape for the match. I told my friend we would watch the highlights when we got back in. So my wife, daughter, friend and I all went to the match. We returned home and I let my friend in first, and although it was pretty traumatic at the time, looking back, it seemed like a sketch from *The Fast Show*.

'Check to see if the match taped?' I shouted to him.

'No, it didn't tape,' he replied.

'How is that?'

'Because it didn't.'

'Why not?'

'Because there is no video!'

I'm thinking, what? 'What do you mean, there is no video?'

'There is no video. You don't even have a television! You don't have a video or a television, Pav!'

I thought my friend was taking the piss. But then I switched on the lights and saw everything was gone. It was as if a plague of locusts had been let loose and they'd devoured everything. The house wasn't smashed up or anything but they took all of our clothes, TV and video, although the microwave was left in the middle of the garden at the back, next to a pair of socks. I think they were using the socks as gloves to hide finger prints. I'm guessing they were still in the house when we came home and dashed through the back and over the fence. After that my wife didn't feel safe in the house with our little girl, especially with me being out all day, so we bought a house at 2 Hownan Close, Gosforth.

The house at Darras Hall was great but it was too big and the nature of the housing estate meant we were cut off from everyone. All of the houses were detached and there were big high fences, fern trees or Leylandii fencing you in and keeping people out. This was no good for my young daughter, Vendy, or my wife who were cut off from the world.

It looked as if we were going to be relegated to the third tier of the football league for the first time in the club's history while Ossie was in charge. Kevin came in for the last 16 games of the season and the impact was immediate because we beat Bristol City 3-0 at home in his first game in charge. He then made Brian Kilcline his first signing, and immediately installed him as club captain. Keegan later remarked that Killer was the most influential signing he had ever made for the club. He was an important signing for us because he was a big personality and crucial in saving the club from relegation and possible bankruptcy, if some stories are to be believed.

Keegan built the team around Killer at the time. Killer would be shouting, screaming and bollocking people on the pitch and everyone took it because they respected him. He was an experienced defender, after all, who had won the FA Cup with Coventry. Obviously I didn't know who he was, but then again, I didn't know much about anything or anyone at that time. I lived in a Communist state for all but one year of my life. In Europe now, players are preparing for life in another country by learning a second or third language and one of them is always English. I only knew Czech and Russian. Kevin Keegan was one of the most famous footballers of his generation and in the world and I didn't know who he was, so it was hardly surprising I didn't know about Killer. But I soon got to know him and what a man he was for us.

Overall the results weren't great. You could feel the tension and atmosphere as the end of the season was closing in on us and we still didn't have enough points to stay up. We won seven, lost seven and drew two of those 16 games and just survived thanks to a dramatic last game of the season at Leicester, where we won 2-1.

David Kelly was a great friend to me. He was always asking whether I was OK or if I wanted anything. Kevin Sheedy was another new signing Keegan brought in to help us beat relegation. He was a terrific lad. He lived near me in Darras Hall and picked me up for training on several occasions. It must have been difficult for him trying to make conversation with someone who didn't speak the language, yet he tried. He would ask, 'You OK Pav? You fit?' and I would just answer everything with a, 'Yeah, yeah, everything good.' I can laugh about it now but it must have been difficult for him and the others. I have some nice memories of those lads.

Yet the Special K show was nearly over before it started when Keegan walked out after we had beaten Glenn Hoddle's Swindon Town 3-1. We felt we were just about to turn things around after a mixed bag of results under Kevin. Only four days earlier we had been down to Cambridge United and won 2-0. The U's were a big tough side who played route one football, back then. We managed to nullify the threat of Dion Dublin that evening and win. The home victory over Swindon meant we had won four, drawn one and lost only two since Kevin arrived.

We were all shocked when we heard he'd walked out on the club. It turns out Kevin was trying to buy a player and Sir John Hall either wouldn't sanction it or couldn't raise the money. Some said it was Swindon's David Kerslake but I'm sure it was Bez, John Beresford. I remember Kevin's famous comment of, 'It's not like it read in the brochure.' After the Swindon game, Kevin walked into the dressing room and said: 'Good luck lads. This isn't about you.' The chairman eventually resolved the problem by flying down to the south coast, or maybe it was Majorca, where Keegan had a house, to talk him around, so he was back before we knew it. There were rumours flying around at the time that Kevin was always throwing a tantrum and behaving like a little boy to get his own way but we had never seen that side of him.

Later on Kevin had a fantastic position in the club with regards to getting what player he wanted. I believe that walk-out episode strengthened that standing and worked in his favour. I think Sir John was maybe frightened he would walk out again, so he bought every player Kevin asked for. No more so, later on, than when he signed Andy Cole and then Alan Shearer for a world record fee of £15m. This said a lot about Keegan. It was as if he was saying, 'You want me to stay? Then you need to go and sign this player and that player otherwise I will walk away.' He seemed to be a master at manipulating a situation.

When he came back to training the following Monday nothing was really said, to my memory. We just carried on where he left off; although, not long after, our results started to suffer and take a turn for the worse. We drew 1-1 away at Grimsby, and beat our fierce rivals Sunderland 1-0 at St James' Park in the following two matches before five defeats in a row left us on the brink of relegation. But a tremendous strike from Ned Kelly in a 1-0 triumph over Portsmouth, and my old boss, Jim Smith, gave us three valuable points. We followed up that with a nail-biting 2-1 victory over Leicester in the last fixture of the season to stay up. As it happens we didn't need to win that day. But we weren't to know the other results were going to go in our favour. Gavin Peacock put us ahead in the first half and the game just seemed to drag on from then. Steve Walsh equalised in injury time before putting one in his own goal only a minute later. It was *Roy of the Rovers* stuff. I didn't understand the gravity of the club's situation until later. It goes without saying it was a relief to stay up. Who knows what would've happened had we gone down?

But when I look back now, I wasn't really involved much, other than the game against Tranmere. I watched everything from afar, trying to take it all in. At the end of the season there was no get-together. Kevin didn't get us all together and talk about the new campaign, probably because his contract was only a short-term deal until the end of the season. He, like us, didn't know whether he was going to be in charge the following campaign. I remember getting a letter from the club saying I had to report back for training. When I checked the date, we had eight weeks off. In the

Czech Republic, we got two weeks off and then we were back to work. I didn't know what to do with all that free time.

I still didn't know where I stood at United. I hadn't established myself as the club's number one. A lot of other people would've just thrown in the towel and decided not to return for the following season. But I was a proud man; proud of where I was from in the Czech Republic. I felt I was representing my nation, and if I did quit, I would've been seen as a failure by the people of my country. Also, I didn't want to let my family down.

Everything was a struggle for me, though: language, life and culture in general. Of course, Pavla, my wife, wanted to return to the Czech Republic the whole time. She did learn to love Newcastle. But she missed her family and spent most of her time on the phone, so I had that extra pressure. I was trying to settle in and obviously the injury I sustained didn't help matters. In one year at the club we had three managers: Jim Smith, Ossie Ardiles and Kevin Keegan. It did make me stronger in the long term, I know that now. And maybe being a young man I was probably a bit sensitive. Nevertheless, I was more determined than ever to prove myself after an injury-plagued season.

CHAPTER 5
GOT THE T-SHIRT

There was no real hint of what was to come when we returned for pre-season training. Kevin was giving interviews prior to the curtain raiser against Southend, stating he was confident Newcastle could challenge Manchester United for the Premier League title. When you consider we survived the previous campaign by the skin of our teeth that was an extraordinary statement. Anyone other than Keegan making statements like that you would think they'd been taking drugs! I thought maybe consolidation or a place in the play-offs might have been a more realistic target. But hats off to the gaffer; it was champagne stuff all the way.

I had learned my lesson from the previous pre-season and went back fitter after the break. But it didn't matter, I was still physically sick at the Maiden Castle training ground. Once again, Tommy Wright was the fittest and fastest out of the group. He was laughing at us all. I remember in one session I literally thought I was going to die. My heart was pounding, trying to escape from my body and run away. That's what it felt like. Then after we finished our final run, someone shouted for us to run one more lap. I would have held a bit back if I knew there was going to be another circuit, but I didn't. I put everything into that previous lap. I did manage to do it without dying, thankfully. It wasn't that I was overweight or unfit; it's just that I was never involved in any training at that level of intensity before. Yes, we did running in the

Czech Republic, but not on this scale; and certainly not the goalkeepers.

In pre-season Kevin signed Paul Bracewell from arch rivals Sunderland for £250,000, and Barry Venison from Liverpool for the same fee. Venners was a steal at that price but he was deemed surplus to requirements by Anfield chief Graeme Souness, who was doing a similar rebuilding job on Merseyside to the one Kevin was doing on Tyneside. Keegan finally landed John Beresford, who had caught his eye during Portsmouth's run to the FA Cup semi-final the previous season. It had looked as if he was going to sign for Liverpool, until he failed the medical. There was no problem passing a medical at St James' Park, if my experience was anything to go by.

It was a new look side to the one which had flirted with relegation the previous season, and there was a good blend of youth and experience. Kevin converted Steve Howey from a striker to a centre half while Killer and Kevin Scott also provided experience at the back with Venners. Kevin Brock had a good head on his shoulders, while Kevin Sheedy had seen it all and got the T-shirt. Lee Clark was arguably the rising young star in the camp, with Robbie Elliott, Steve Watson and Alan Thompson also showing promise, while the veterans Brace, Sheedy and Liam O'Brien added their know-how in the middle of midfield. And up front there wasn't a better front pairing in the division than David Kelly and Gavin Peacock. They dovetailed together beautifully. Gavin would drop deep in the hole while Ned was happy running in the channels.

Micky Quinn got his nose pushed out of joint and said some unsavoury things when he left, but admitted later regretting saying them. I was aware of the problems he was having with Kevin because everyone was saying what a great player he was. He had a great record as a striker. But Quinny was getting older and starting to lose the sharpness he'd had as a younger player. So Kevin moved him onto Coventry because Quinny wanted to play every week and wouldn't accept being a squad player.

Keegan did the same with Franz Carr, who I think was only the second or third black player to have played for the Magpies. This was also the first time I shared a dressing room with a black player. I never got the opportunity because there were no black players in the Czech Republic. He always drove a black BMW and when he opened the boot there were these massive speakers in there.

He said, 'Look at this, Pav.'

I'd never seen anything like it in my life. The music he played was awful, an almost deafening racket. I'm saying, 'Howay, Franz, give me a break.'

And he's going, 'No, Pav, this is great.' He loved his cars. Nothing ever seemed to get him down. If he wasn't in the team, he would shrug his shoulders. If he was in the team, then he would shrug his shoulders. He never showed any emotion so I don't know whether it bothered him being in the side or not.

Ned Kelly was also moved on by Kevin the season after, which shocked me, given all he had done for the team. Ned came to see me and said he was leaving the club. This was unusual because players rarely confided in others they were leaving. One day they would be there, the next they were gone. There was no bitterness from Ned at all. He accepted Keegan's honesty that he would be buying bigger and better players to take the club on to greater heights. But that was Ned's career. He moved around a lot. He never stopped at a club for more than two or three years. What a job he did for Newcastle. He used to bust a gut in every game. Keegan used to appreciate players like that, giving 100 per cent for the cause. And Ned was great with me. I appreciated everything he did. Every time we see each other I get a big hug and we reminisce over the old times. He was, and still is, great craic.

Keegan seemed to have a knack of getting the most out of his players, and when he couldn't extract any more out them they would be shipped out. He was also preparing for life in the top flight and knew he had to keep refreshing the squad and adding better players. Kevin Sheedy did a great job helping to keep us up in 1992 and was instrumental in the great start we had in our promotion year. But then a younger model arrived in the shape of Scott Sellars and Sheedy left as well. Another surprise was the transfer of Gavin Peacock to Chelsea for £1.5m. Although maybe I shouldn't have been surprised because I knew Gavin's wife hadn't settled. His son had been born with part of his arm missing and they wanted to be closer to their family.

Keegan did this with Andy Cole as well. I reckon he was born with that instinct of knowing when it was right to get rid of a player. But when a new player arrived at the club everyone got excited, even more so when it was an unknown like Coley. Keegan had paid £1.75m for him from Bristol City; a lot of money for an untested talent. Yet Kevin never seemed to buy a bad player, so we knew he must have secured something special. You could see in training, immediately, that we had captured an exciting new talent. He was fast, great movement and, of course, an eye for goal.

I got on really well with Andy at first but then we fell out after a game at Coventry. He wasn't having a good game and we got a penalty. Andy grabbed the ball and walked towards the penalty spot and planted it down. I shouted towards the dugout to tell the boss that he shouldn't take it because his confidence was low. He missed the kick so my first instinct was correct.

When I got to the dressing room after the game it all kicked off into an almighty row because I told him he shouldn't have taken the spot kick. Andy told me to fuck off. I tried to explain but he didn't want to know and from that day on he didn't really talk to me. Keegan gave me a right bollocking afterwards.

'It's not your place to say who can and who can't take the penalties, it's mine. You do your job,' he said.

'I did my job by keeping a clean sheet,' I replied.

I was incensed but then Arthur Cox intervened and got between us and took me away. But passions were high after game and you say things in the heat of the moment.

There were always big personalities in our dressing room. I was upset because we should've won the game instead of coming away with a point. I think it is healthy to get things out in the open and clear the air; then after the game go and have a drink. All of that aside, Andy Cole was a fantastic player for us and went on to bigger and better things.

I got my head down during pre-season training and worked hard. I played in a couple of the friendlies prior to the new term but it was still unclear who would start the season. Tommy finished the last campaign in goal so I expected it would be him who would start the new season as the club's number one. Now that I'm a coach I tell my goalkeepers at the start of every new term who will be my number one, two and three, so they know where they stand. I tell them it could change during the season but that's what I do because that is what I would've liked when I played. Keegan and Dalglish never said that to any of their goalkeepers. You need to know because you mentally prepare differently for each role: one, two and three. Number one plays, number two is on the bench and number three is in the stands. I remember talking to Kevin about a new contract after we got promoted to the Premier League. He said we cannot give you more than what I asked for. I can't remember what the number was at the time. I was disappointed with the offer, so asked why. He said, 'You and Tommy Wright are on a level pegging and I want the goalkeepers on the same salary.' I said I wasn't interested with what Tommy got; I was only interested in my salary.

Tommy was the manager's preferred choice at the beginning of the season as we won the first 11 games. I felt like a passenger or an outsider. The team were playing fantastic football but I wasn't involved, so I felt a little left out. I didn't get a look in until a 0-0 home draw with Swindon in November. Tommy got injured in the 3-2 win at Birmingham in the previous fixture. It was the game where Kevin Brock went in goal because Kevin didn't put a goalkeeper on the bench. It was a time when you could have two substitutes. It was also the game where former chairman Stan Seymour had a heart attack and later died. There was no point banging on the gaffer's door demanding to play because, to be fair to Tommy, he did play well when we went on that fantastic run. He was unlucky to get injured. Despite that, I still hated being number two.

The back pass rule came into effect in the 1992 season. It was brought in to discourage time-wasting and overly defensive play and to combat time-stalling techniques, which happened to stifle the 1990 World Cup in Italy. Goalkeepers were no longer allowed to roll the ball and pick it up either. Once the ball was released to the floor you had to kick or pass it. You could only hold the ball for five seconds as well once it was under control. This may have speeded up the game but it made a goalkeeper's job more difficult. I came into my own when this rule was introduced because I was more comfortable with the ball at my feet than most goalkeepers. I remember a comment made by Leicester manager Brian Little earlier that season. We had played City in the Anglo Italian Cup and beat them 4-0 at St James' Park. The Foxes boss jokingly quipped he was thinking about putting a transfer bid in for me, as a striker! Little had been impressed with my footwork in the game.

Kevin made the unusual step of bringing in Jimmy Montgomery as the club's goalkeeping coach. Unusual because Monty was a Sunderland legend and the Black Cats were our fierce rivals. It was typical Kevin though. If you were deemed good enough to be involved with us it didn't matter where you came from.

If I remember rightly, it caused more of a fuss on Wearside than it did on Tyneside. Sunderland supporters were outraged their own club couldn't find a role for their former hero yet their sworn enemies could.

I really enjoyed working with Jimmy. He was a Sunderland legend and rightly so. He used to talk about his playing days; in particular the 1960s side he played for. Obviously we spoke about his famous save against Leeds in the 1973 FA Cup final and how good the banter was in his heyday. Monty used to drive me in to training and supporters used to stand by the goal and watch us and listen to his patter. I used to love sharing the passion and knowledge we had with those supporters standing around watching us as well. It wasn't just about the 90 minutes on a Saturday because not everyone could get into the stadium. You have to give Keegan some credit for that. Jimmy wasn't with us very long because a role was eventually found for one of Sunderland's favourite sons. It must have been tough for those followers south of the Tyne seeing one of their own help improve the team of their bitter enemies, while their fortunes floundered. Monty was a great coach and I missed him when he left.

I had a great season after that and claimed the first team goalkeeper's jersey as my own. I kept 13 clean sheets in 32 games as we steamrollered most of the opposition who stood in our way and won the championship at a canter. We had fun, there was a great feeling we were doing something special and I thought I'd done more than enough to cement my place as the club's number one goalkeeper. And when I got in I thought my spell between the posts after

Tommy got injured was just as good if not better than the Irishman's efforts. I had an unswerving belief I was the best goalkeeper at the club. But not only did I think that, several of the players used to tell me, which obviously fuelled my self-belief.

It was the little things at first, such as the first team picking players in training for the six and seven-a-side games. I would always get picked first. They would say, 'I'll take Pav.' Why would they do that? They want to win. Venners, David Kelly and Bez, especially at that time, used to tell me I was the best. Not so much Paul Bracewell, who was very sarcastic. I thought he was having a go at me but then I found out he was like that with everyone. Later on Rob Lee had time for me and Pedro obviously. It gave you a tremendous boost.

There was this one time the following season when Kevin called me into his office at Maiden Castle and told me I was going to play at Blackburn. We lost the game 1-0 but I remember I played well. The following morning I passed Bez, in the corridor, and as he walked by me he said, 'Well done, Pav. We have the best goalkeeper in the league.' I thought he didn't need to say that. He could've just walked past me. Yet he did say it and wanted to tell me. Things like that, words of encouragement kept me going when I was out of the first team picture.

It was a great time for the team, the fans and the city of Newcastle. The camaraderie in the dressing room was incredible. It wasn't one person, although Ned seemed to be at the centre of a lot of banter. We all bounced off one another. One person would say something, another would add to it and then we would all fall about laughing. Not every club I played for had this togetherness. At the time, I didn't realise that this was as special as it was, until after I left the club.

Credit must also go to Sir John Hall, as well, because he was the man with the money bringing in players. It was a great combination between Keegan and Hall. Hall trusted Keegan's intuition and instinct for players and he was rewarded for that. He used to come down into the changing room every now and again, shake all the players' hands and wish us good luck. He would jokingly ask how the Czech currency was doing and added that I must be a happy man with the wages I was getting. There was never any pressure on the manager asking why this player or that player wasn't playing. It is different in Italy and the Czech Republic. The chairmen are buying the players and interfere with team selection. They want to know why their favourites aren't playing and why the team isn't playing a certain way. Sir John never did any of that. He trusted Kevin to get on with his job. You have to give him credit for that. Every year Sir John would have a party in his house for all the players and their families and it was great fun. I couldn't see the owners or chairmen of other clubs doing the same.

We played an open expansive game with flair and passion. Everybody was pulling in the same direction. We wanted the Division One title and no one was going to stand in our way until we got it. It was fantastic to be a part of that group. The confidence kept building up to almost unassailable levels. We felt invincible that season. And with the crowd behind us, it was amazing. I still believe those 36,000 supporters we were pulling in back then were louder than the

52,000 that go today. The passion and noise they generated was astonishing. Obviously I'm not being disrespectful to the supporters who go now, but it seemed those 36,000 were more thunderous and deafening. You could feel and almost touch the atmosphere when you ran on to the pitch in the stadium. The hairs on the back on my neck used to stand up. My heart would be pumping and it would get the adrenaline going. I used to thrive on it. In fact every time I think back to those days it gives me goose bumps.

I remember reading somewhere that Killer said the favourite time of his career was at Newcastle, yet he lifted the FA Cup as captain of Coventry in 1987. Killer hardly played for us because Steve Howey was emerging as a fine young centre half. But Killer thrived on the banter. He loved coming into training every morning, he loved the lads and having a drink with them. He was always supportive to everyone who played. He had a fantastic attitude. There was a television interview a few days after we clinched promotion to the Premier League, with Keegan, Ned and a couple of others. Killer asked Kevin in front of the cameras if he could have a more comfortable cushion to sit on in the dugout for forthcoming season. That was the measure of the man, always laughing and joking.

I've noticed a few things have changed from back then as well. Now, it seems supporters just turn up ten minutes before the game. When I played the stadium used to be full when we were warming up and making a racket before we'd even kicked off. Of course, now, there is more traffic and perhaps it takes longer for people to get in to the ground the way it is set up. So this is maybe understandable. I think the passion has been lost somewhere. Maybe it is the way the club has been run recently though.

Sparta Prague played away at Chelsea recently and the Sparta fans were fantastic but the Blues' supporters were all quiet. The Sparta players were asking, 'How is this possible when Chelsea are the best team in England?' I would tell them that this isn't how it was when I played at Newcastle United. At Maiden Castle, there was between 3,000 and 4,000 fans watching us every day. They would come with their sandwiches, tea and coffee and I would stay behind half an hour after training and shake most of their hands. It was the happiest time of my life. I would teach the kids a little bit after training, if they wanted, or sign autographs. It was an absolute pleasure for me. When I tell people about this time at Newcastle they don't believe it. We had more supporters at training than go to games in Czech Republic.

Then we had a party against Leicester on the last day of the season. But it still rankles with me the goal the Foxes scored from a free-kick. There was no referee's whistle. I was lining up the wall and a City player chipped it in when I wasn't ready. I know United supporters might laugh at this, because we played champagne football that day, but as a goalkeeper you scrutinise every goal you concede and I am no different. Ned Kelly and Andy Cole both bagged a hat-trick in our 7-1 triumph, with Robert Lee adding the other.

That aside, I knew I had won the fans around after that game in particular. In the past they may have shouted 'dodgy keeper', but not any more. Instead, if I made a mistake, supporters got behind me rather than having a go. They were shouting, 'Pav, keep your head up,' and 'Come on, Pav, don't worry about it,' which was nice. I can remember the last time someone shouted 'dodgy keeper' but it wasn't at a game. Three teenagers shouted it at me outside the ground. It may have been an ironic chant or even some Sunderland supporters, I don't know. But I never heard it inside a stadium after our Division One championship win.

The *Pavel is a Geordie* t-shirt is a well known story now. Lee Clark's brother, Michael, gave it to Clarky to pass on to me. Clarky said, 'Wear this and you'll be a Geordie legend.' Looking back it is still a special moment for me, why? It was a symbol of acceptance from the Newcastle supporters. It seemed the fans chanted my name even louder when they saw me wearing it on the pitch for the customary lap of honour after the trophy was presented. I still have it, of course, and when I finally settle down it will go pride of place on a wall in my house. That is how much that t-shirt means to me.

I remember after the game, in the dressing room, we celebrated and had some champagne. Ned Kelly said to me, 'Come on, Pav, walk with me and go back on the pitch and let's enjoy this.' So we went back on the pitch and it was a fantastic feeling. But all of that season was special.

When you take into consideration we were nearly relegated the season before it was a phenomenal achievement. It was a complete turnaround in fortunes. We more or less started with the same squad as the previous term. Venners, Brace and Bez were the only new signings before Rob Lee came in the October. Andy Cole, Scott Sellars and Mark Robinson were added later on to seal the title.

Barry Venison, wasn't the greatest footballer, but he had the heart of a lion, a great motivator and a first class attitude. One of the best professionals I have ever played with. He will die for you on the football pitch. He'd do anything to win a game of football. I loved that about Venners. He was hard but fair and dished out bollockings when they were deserved but also gave praise when it was needed. He never got personal with you. It was for the greater good of the team.

John Beresford was a chirpy kind of chap. He was always laughing and joking and had a smile on his face. He was another good guy in the dressing room. Sometimes you got the feeling he was a bit of a prima donna but then when he got hit he would bounce straight back up. I always got the feeling that Bez not only had time for me as a person but also as a goalkeeper.

We had a great team full of characters but there were no prima donnas or superstars. When we went out, for a meal or a drink, we all went out as a team. What a difference to when I first joined the club when there were little cliques all over the dressing room. We were all in this together, fighting for the same cause.

A couple of hours after the game, celebrations and lap of honour, Pavla and I got in the car and tried to head off for home. I was heading down Percy Street and we stopped at the traffic lights opposite the Three Bulls pub; I think it was called. There were hundreds of supporters out on the streets, having a drink and celebrating. Then one supporter spotted me and shouted, 'It's Pav!' Around 40 supporters ran to the car and started singing, 'Pavel is a Geordie,' while the traffic lights turned from red to green. We couldn't go because the car was surrounded by fans rocking and shaking the vehicle. They tried to lift it from the road and put it on the side. I opened the roof and tried to get the lads to stop and calm down. It was obvious, several drinks had been taken. They were dancing and singing and were in high spirits. Some of them poured drink into the car shouting, 'Pav, have a drink, man!' Pavla, my wife, and Vendy, my daughter, were in the car and were shocked, although they knew they weren't in any danger. The traffic lights changed about five or six times; there were cars backed up behind wondering what was going on, before we eventually got away. No one stuck behind us complained. When they saw what was happening they just laughed. But it was great fun. Everyone was in party mood.

I remember we had a big party at the Civic Centre a few days after we won the league. The streets surrounding the building were chock-a-block with supporters. Thousands of them had turned out to see the bus parade and it was pissing down. They had stopped buses and other traffic getting in and around the Haymarket. Never before had I seen anything like it. The supporters were singing in the rain, chanting all our names and I thought to myself, I've finally found my second home. I had a sense of belonging. I loved the city, the football club and, more importantly, the supporters, and they had taken me to their hearts.

CHAPTER 6
HOOPER CHALLENGE

Tackles were flying in fast and furious. This was normal in our six or seven-a-side training games. They were always competitive, high tempo and there was always a bit of an edge to them. A fired-up Lee Clark had put Keegan on his backside only a few moments earlier and Venners gave it to the gaffer with two barrels: 'You shouldn't be playing with us anymore! You're not good enough!' You could see the boss was visibly shaken by the comment.

The incident was arguably of Keegan's making. Clarky was upset with Kevin about team matters and decided to extract revenge on the boss. A few home truths were spoken around this time. In essence, Venners told Keegan he shouldn't be involved anymore. Instead he should be watching from the sidelines. Keegan loved to play in the training games but his side rarely won. And more often than not, his team generally lost. Barry was annoyed because his side, with Keegan in it, were defeated again. Venners hated losing. He was a winner, even in training. But what the former Liverpool defender said upset Keegan.

I remember the lads taking the piss out of Venners when we got back into the changing room. They were saying, 'Fucking hell, Venners, are you mad?' or, 'That's the last game you're going to play for Newcastle.' But Venners was serious. He meant every word of it and he was right; Keegan wasn't good enough to play at our level anymore. The gaffer, to his credit, never played another game after that. I'm not sure if that was the beginning of the end for Venners, mind, because I know he had a few problems off the pitch. But despite that Keegan still had a lot of respect for him.

I always find it amusing when people criticised Keegan for scraping the reserves. The critics said there was a lack of a competitive edge for the guys not involved with the first team. They should've come down and witnessed our training games and then asked themselves the same question. There was no quarter drawn. They were all full blooded affairs with several players looking to make a point to the gaffer if they weren't in the team.

I'd returned home to the Czech Republic at the end of the previous season. We always had a short holiday when the campaign ended. One year it was St Lucia and another in Cyprus, for example. Then my wife and I would go back to the Czech Republic to see our friends and family for the rest of the time. It was quite stressful returning to my home nation. There were never any direct flights to Prague back in those days. We had to sometimes take two or three flights, involving Amsterdam, Brussels or Paris, to get home. And, when we got home, nine times out of ten, we would get turned over at the airport for taking gifts back. More often than not we had to pay an extra tax on them. Despite the fact Communism was coming to an end the Czech people still had the same mind set. We're thinking is this really worth it? We got more of a break back in Newcastle.

I remember thinking to myself, life is great, despite the hassle of getting home for a holiday. I had just won the league and established myself as the club's number one goalkeeper. I felt euphoric; on top of the world and excited at the prospect of playing in the Premier League, which had just been formed the previous season. We were a young team with several Geordies in the squad, which the fans always appreciated. St James' Park was being redeveloped and taking shape quite nicely off the field and we were ready for a new adventure.

We were quietly confident we would do well in the top flight but never expected to finish quite as high as we did in our first season back in the big time. In hindsight, the second season was harder because we weren't an unknown quantity anymore. We probably got away with a lot in our first season through our naivety.

Yet despite all of the supporters' adulation, performing well and earning the right to be the club's number one, there was never any encouragement from Kevin. I always got the feeling he wanted me out and was looking for a replacement. I was the only player he had never signed and he always coveted his own men, not someone else's players. I don't think Terry Mac rated me either. I'm not sure whether there was any influence from Kevin. He was another who never gave me any praise or singled me out when I played well. There were a few games when I kept a clean sheet and they would both say, 'But you didn't have much to do.' I would never say that to my goalkeepers. I know now from experience making comments like that is not good for confidence. It is the same when the pundits start hammering the goalkeepers. They have never played the position so how can they comment?

How can they understand? They don't have the empathy. Goalkeeping is a specialist position.

There used to be a bit of banter in the dressing room about potential players coming to the club. One player would mention who we were being linked with and then another would say that the player, we were supposedly targeting, was shite, and so on. Or on other occasions one of the players would know the guy and would say whether he was a good bloke or not. There was talk of us signing Mike Hooper when we were back in pre-season training. And sure enough Kevin signed him a month into the new campaign. Mike was not just brought in for competition for me, but as the club's number one goalkeeper. Can you imagine how I felt?

This was the story of my life at Newcastle. It didn't matter how many times I got in the team and played well, it wasn't good enough. There were 36,000 fans who knew I was the best goalkeeper at the club, yet the man who picked the team didn't like it. I thought I was winning the fight but losing the battle against Kevin because it seemed he didn't like to be proved wrong. When Mike arrived I thought, Jesus, he must be some goalkeeper to be better than me. I'll have to try and up my game and be at my best. But no disrespect to Mike, because he was a good keeper, I didn't think he was better than me. When I saw him in training I thought he was overweight; he couldn't dive on the left side; but he was a strong kicker of the ball. Maybe Kevin thought Mike would be better at handling crosses than me, which wasn't one of my strong points when I first arrived in England.

I liked Mike as a person. He was a good guy, polite and very helpful. He didn't cover himself in glory and soon after he arrived the fans were hostile towards him. He even spoke with me about it, put his hands up and admitted he wasn't playing well. He actually confessed he was relieved when he was eventually dropped because he let me know he was struggling like he'd never struggled before. I'm not sure if he was having problems with his wife at home. One day she turned up at the training ground at Maiden Castle. She drove his sponsored dark red Rover car over the training pitches like she was in a James Bond movie. She got out and screamed, 'Where's my fucking money?' I was thinking, fucking hell, what is going on here? I was scared, but Mike was calm in the situation. He told her to take it easy but she was yelling, 'I'll not take it easy. Where's my fucking money!' He said she would get her money. I didn't like to ask what it was about because it was none of my business. But I felt embarrassed for the two of them.

Mike was an unusual guy. He kept a menagerie of animals. He had bull mastiff dogs; snakes; tarantulas and other exotic spiders. He also had a Great Dane. I nearly shit myself when I first went to his house and I saw this dog with a massive head standing with his paws on the six foot garden fence, looking at me. He let the dog in and it jumped up at me, paws on my shoulders. I'm saying, 'Mike, what's happening?' He says, 'Don't worry, Pav, he's a nice dog.' Well, I'm 6ft 2in, but the dog was taller than me when it stood on its two hind legs. But the other dogs, I'm not sure if they were Bull Mastiffs, Bull Dogs or other fighting dogs. Mike says, 'Don't even look at the little one; he's a nasty little bastard.' He always said when he finished playing football he wanted to have a farm.

Hoops also suffered from Tourettes. There were times when we would be talking, or in a formal situation, and he would start swearing or say something inappropriate. We would all fall about laughing when this happened. Yet he was an incredibly intelligent man and I believe he had an English degree. He was always playing Scrabble with Keegan on the bus to and from away games.

Mike never made a fuss or complained when he got dropped and couldn't get back in the side. When Keegan left him out the team him he came to seek me out. He shook my hand and wished me good luck. He was disappointed, you could see that but he was honourable with it. I remember we played at Liverpool and won 2-0. I played well that day. A few days later he picked me up for training and he was very complimentary about my performance. He said, 'Pav, you were fantastic. You had a great game against my old club.' These words came from a man whose place I'd taken in the side not long before. He didn't have to say it but it says a lot about the man. He had integrity and grace. I liked Mike a lot. He was a nice man and had something special about him. I'm sorry his football career did not turn out the way he wanted.

I started the new season in goal where we lost 1-0 at home in the campaign's curtain raiser against my old boss, Ossie Ardlies, and his Tottenham side. The game was a bit of an anticlimax. We just didn't perform and Teddy Sheringham netted the only goal of the game.

We then travelled to Coventry. I got sent off for bringing down Roy Wegerle and my old team mate,

Micky Quinn, blazed the ball over the bar from the spot. We had taken a 1-0 lead after Liam O'Brien's free-kick was deflected in. But goals from Peter Ndlovu and a header from Mick Harford gave them the three points. It is fair to say we had a stuttering start to life in the Premier League. A hard-earned point at Old Trafford against last season's champions was the start of our turnaround. Ryan Giggs put one past me with a 20 yards free-kick, which I got a hand too, before Coley levelled it for us.

We hadn't yet been christened the Entertainers but we were fast beginning to earn the moniker. We seemed to be everybody's second favourite team and everyone loved the way we played our football, which was very exciting for us as a team and squad as well. I'm guessing the British public hadn't seen anything as refreshing as our style of football for a long time. But we just kept the momentum going from the previous promotion season and carried it on during our first campaign in the Premier League.

Kevin kept adding quality players to the squad as we went along and that helped; no one more so than Peter Beardsley. I remember everyone questioning whether we should be paying £1.5m for player in his early thirties. Some of the tricks he would pull off, the little bits of magic and genius were a joy to watch. There was a buzz about the place when we knew he was returning home. It was a crushing blow to lose Peter on the eve of the season. He fractured his cheek bone in a friendly at Liverpool after a challenge from Neil Ruddock, who scored the winning goal in a 1-0 win. There was a lot of bad feeling because Beardsley felt the Reds centre half did it on purpose.

But when Pedro returned to the side he struck up an immediate rapport with Andy Cole. It was a fantastic strike partnership, almost telepathic. Pedro would drop off short, Coley would set off and the little fella would find him with a slide rule pass, nine times out of ten. It was one of the best combinations, if not the best, I'd ever had the privilege to play with. Andy netted 41 times and broke the goal scoring record of Newcastle folk hero and legend Hughie Gallagher. Meanwhile, Pedro helped himself to 24 goals, as well as setting up most of his partner's strikes.

None of Pedro's goals were tap ins, either. They were from 20 yards; 30 yards; mazy dribbles; left foot and right foot. They were all different. It was exciting to watch! He always gave 100 per cent, even in training. I remember when we used to play five-a-side. The player who had the biggest stinker out of the lot of us got the yellow shirt; Pedro never received it. So, after a while, the lads got together and conspired to vote for him as a joke. He was furious. Not happy at all. He called us all of the swear words under the sun because, he knew, as we did, he didn't deserve it. He threw the shirt on the floor and refused to wear it and we all fell about laughing. It was great fun. But all joking aside, Pedro was a fantastic man, incredible person and a dedicated professional. One of the best I've had the fortune to play with.

Budgie returned to us as well. It was great to see him back at the club. He acted as cover but mainly as a coach. He used to set up the sessions for the goalkeepers. I always got the feeling he was putting them on for himself, rather than for me, Mike or Tommy, who left for Nottingham Forest that term.

There were times when I felt Kevin ignored me, maybe because I hadn't yet mastered the English language. There were other times when he was very sarcastic towards me. Him and Terry Mac, always used to talk about the medals they had won. Kevin would say, 'Terry, remember when we won this trophy and that trophy?' Then they would start laughing. We would be thinking, what? We had won fuck all. Maybe they were saying it to try to get us to achieve and reach the same heights or goals they had as players, I don't know. But the players hated it. If a new player had come to the club and behaved like that we would have told them to fuck off.

At Southampton the gaffer substituted Lee Clark and he was furious with Kevin. Clarky kicked over a bucket of water by the dugout, told Keegan to fuck off and started to walk off towards the tunnel. This infuriated the boss because not only did he tell him where to go but it was being televised, so the whole nation was watching it. Kevin wasn't one of those managers who shouted and screamed at his players. He used to raise his voice every now and again but there was no hair dryer treatment, like Sir Alex Ferguson. The bus journey home was no different to any other trip after we lost, which was always quiet.

People have often said that when you cross Kevin he never forgives nor forgets and maybe that was my problem. I never gave up and I always fought my corner. Most of the players and fans were also behind me. I'm not sure Kevin liked that. Mike Hooper had come under pressure from the fans because he wasn't playing very well. Kevin made a big point in the newspapers of saying he picks the team and not the fans. But if the fans want him to go he would. It was a bit like the Andy Cole situation when he confronted fans on the stairs at St James' Park. He hated being proved wrong and I was proving him wrong. I don't think he liked that.

Andy Cole was having different problems settling in. I'm not sure how it worked out but the club found him somewhere to live in Crook. It was strange because it was a bit out of the way and none of the other players lived there. Andy was a proud man with a strong personality and felt intensely about his position. Kevin and Andy had had a few choice words in training which resulted in our record signing going AWOL.

Andy wasn't the best trainer when he arrived at Newcastle. He didn't try very hard, although that did change later on. I think his performances on the pitch were the main thing and he always played well in general. Kevin was frustrated with Andy because he didn't give it his all in training as well. Mind you, Pedro always said the Newcastle training sessions were tougher than anything he'd ever encountered at Everton or Liverpool and he'd won trophies with them. Training was very intense and I loved it. I always tell my goalkeepers if you have the right attitude you can go far. If you don't have the right attitude you'll get nowhere. I brought this word from England, based on my time at Newcastle. And I use the English word, attitude, rather than translating it into Czech, so they remember it. No one can ever accuse me of not giving 100 per cent. If they did I would probably retire. I might not have been the greatest goalkeeper in the world but I always give it my best. I have been like that all my life pushing myself through the pain barrier.

It is expected that a player and the manager or coaches will not see eye to eye on occasion. It is normal. I never thought the situation with Coley or Clarky would fester and cause problems in the future. It was all sorted out very quickly and we moved on. Of course players are unhappy when they aren't playing or there is a domestic situation but that's life. In general we always had a happy dressing room. There weren't any bad eggs in my time there. In fact, other than seeing Budgie and Chris Guthie, our kit man, going hammer and tongs at each other, I never saw a physical fight between any of our players. I'm not even sure what that was about, although Budgie could be a bit feisty at times.

There was that incident in training involving Lee Clark and the gaffer when Clarky took him out. So to diffuse the situation I dashed out of goal, screamed and high kicked above Clarky's head. He was shocked but it had the effect I wanted because it stopped him in his tracks. Kevin pulled up Clarky about the clash in the dressing room after training. He told him he couldn't do that because he is the boss and he has to respect he is the manager. Clarky, to his credit, did apologise.

I didn't want to cause any problems for the gaffer but I believed in my own ability. No disrespect to any goalkeeper who arrived on Tyneside during my time at the club, but I didn't think any of them were any better than I was. Looking back, maybe that's why Newcastle fans like me and call me a legend, because I stood up for myself and proved doubters wrong. I am not saying I was the greatest goalkeeper Newcastle ever had, far from it. But I must have done something right. There are more famous and better players than me who have worn the famous black and white jersey, yet they haven't had the respect afforded to me on Tyneside. I think the United fans knew I was honest and hard working and did my best for the club. It gives me a great deal of pleasure and satisfaction that they appreciate what I did. I have a great affection and bond with the people of Newcastle. I just wish I could've played 400 or 500 games for the club, won the supporters a trophy and maybe earned a bit more money, because all of these things go together.

I don't have the same respect, bond or love from the Czech people. Why? One, they don't really know me and secondly the supporters are unforgiving if you have played for the team of their rivals. For instance, Slavia Prague hate me because I am a coach at Sparta Prague, while Sparta fans don't like me because I played for Banik Ostrava. Yes, I played nearly 50 times for my country but I was in and out of the team all of the time, unlike Pavel Nedved, Petr Cech, Tomas Rosicky or Jan Koller. Furthermore, people in the Czech Republic were poor and couldn't afford satellite television or Sky. So many people in the Czech Republic were unaware of who I was or what I was doing. It could've been different mind you. I nearly played in the 1996 European Championships final at Wembley against Germany. I was almost selected for the entire tournament.

One of the Czech goalkeeping coaches only told me this, a few years ago, that the manager and other coaches discussed dropping Petr Kouba for the final. This could've changed my life in the same way had we won the Premier League title that year. But this is the story of my life. I don't want to sound like I am crying over spilt milk or that I am bitter, because I am not. Despite all of the setbacks I've suffered in my career I have a lot to thank football for. I have had a good career. Looking back I am quite philosophical about it. Yes I have a few regrets, everyone does. I should've made a lot of money out of the game but it wasn't to be. I lost my family because I came back to Newcastle and my wife didn't want to come with me and I was ever so close to winning the Premier League and a European Championship.

After our slow start to the campaign we picked up and were flying. We'd climbed to the dizzy heights of third in the league until a couple of setbacks threatened to unrail the season. Two magnificent Matt le Tissier goals had seen us lose 2-1 at The Dell. In truth we had actually battered them; just couldn't find the target that day. We followed up that by crashing out of FA Cup in the fourth round to Luton Town after the Hatters had drawn at our place 1-1. The third defeat came when we were beaten 4-2 at Wimbledon.

Kevin called me into his office the week after we had lost to the Wombles. But when I saw him he looked really sad and depressed. I thought someone had died, seriously! He turned to see me and said, 'Pav, you're playing tomorrow.' The gaffer seemed really disappointed he had to put me back in goal. Mike had come under a lot of pressure prior to that game because he hadn't been playing well and his form was poor. I think Kevin should share some of the blame because he should have taken him out of the firing line earlier. Kevin could be a stubborn so and so and the more people were calling for Mike to be dropped and reinstate me, the more he would ignore them and dig his heels in. I wasn't expecting the recall to be honest because this was a Friday. We generally knew the team on the Wednesday before a weekend match. I should've been happy that I was back in the team but I was upset by Keegan's reaction. We lost 1-0 at Blackburn but the team and I played well. The day after, Bez saw me and said great to have the best goalkeeper in the club back in goal.

Kevin criticised me when he felt I was at fault for a goal, every now and again. However, it was never his style to openly slam his players in public or in front of the other lads. Don't get me wrong, harsh words were spoken on occasions. He would just sign another player who felt was better than the man in possession of the jersey. And that's what he tried to do with me. He was always looking to strengthen the team and make the squad stronger. I didn't feel the need to work any harder because I was doing more than enough to keep my place in the team.

We struggled early on in the season, losing by the odd goal, but we were never hammered. It just took a while for us to find our feet, settle and get used to playing in the top flight. We never had many experienced Premier League players. We had Pedro, but he was a striker. We never had any seasoned defenders, other than Barry Venison, who would say 'slow it down' or 'tuck in and take it easy'. Kevin Scott and Steve Howey were good defenders but they were still kids. They didn't have the old school know-how of a Steve Bruce and Gary Pallister. Darren

Peacock had played a lot of top flight football, but he didn't arrive at the club until the following February, while Ruel Fox came to the club a month earlier. A lot of the time the full backs were bombing on and we were being exposed at the back, because of it. Then I would get criticised off Kevin because of the risks I was taking. But I was playing as a sweeper as well. It was a Catch 22 situation: damned if I do take risks, damned if I don't take risks.

I played the last 15 games of the season but after the reversal at Ewood Park, we lost only two more fixtures. I kept seven clean sheets and conceded 12 times as we finished the season on a high by claiming third position and a place in next season's UEFA Cup. I played 22 matches altogether keeping clean sheets in eight fixtures.

I win the number one jersey again and it's the same old story. It didn't matter what I did, Kevin was always on the lookout for a new goalkeeper. I tried to just keep my head down and work hard but there were times when I just got fed up with the situation. The goalkeeper would be changed and I'm thinking, am I going to save his arse when it goes wrong again? If you look at all of the teams who had success, Manchester United, Arsenal, Liverpool and, later on, Chelsea, they all stuck with the same goalkeeper. Another season closes and I see off another goalkeeper. John Burridge, Tommy Wright and now Mike Hooper have all challenged me for the number one jersey. As the season drew to a close, I remember thinking, I wonder if Kevin will sign another goalkeeper next season?

CHAPTER 7
COLE'S GOALS GONE

Andy Cole's transfer was a massive shock to, not only Newcastle supporters, but to us players as well. It rocked the club to its very foundations. There was no hint or clue that he was looking to move. I know he had a fall out with the gaffer before a League Cup tie at Wimbledon the previous season but we thought that was all water under the bridge. We had the best striker in the Premier League at the time. He had scored 41 goals for us in the last campaign and I'm thinking, who else is going to score the goals now he has left? I was at home when I found out. Andy was missing from training that day but that was nothing unusual. He'd often missed a training session. The squad worked out as normal that day; had lunch at the training ground and then we all went our separate ways, like we always did. I turned on the news later that night and I saw Kevin confront angry supporters on the steps of St James' Park explaining why he had sold Andy.

The club received something like £7m and got Keith Gillespie in exchange as well. That was a lot of money back then. It was the most expensive British transfer fee at the time. I later found out Andy instigated the move with his agent Paul Stretford. I didn't know whether Coley was unhappy at Newcastle; Kevin was unhappy with Andy or whether there were some other politics involved. You could tell he wasn't right. His body language was all wrong and Andy hadn't scored a goal in nearly two months prior to the deal going through; his worst spell at St James' Park.

And when you think about all the flair players we had at the club, it was unusual. It wasn't the Andy Cole we all knew, that's for sure. I had a row with him about taking a penalty we got at Coventry. His body language wasn't good that day. He was poor, and less than a month later he was gone.

As I said earlier, Andy never spoke to me after that and I was disappointed with him. Before that we got on great, laughing and joking. But Andy fell out with a lot of players so I haven't taken it personally. If you look at Andy's record at the beginning of the 1994-95 season he was banging in goals for fun; then they dried up. It was always said, or written, we couldn't defend, yet a month before he departed games were very tight. There were three 0-0 score lines in four games prior to him leaving, while we lost the other 2-1 at Norwich. Notably, Ruel Fox netted from the spot against his old club that day. The same when we lost the title, everyone said we couldn't defend yet we didn't concede many more than Man U. The difference was they scored more goals than us.

I can't remember anything in particular that was said at training the following morning. At the end of the day most professional footballers are selfish and are only concerned about themselves. They are only interested in whether or not they are playing at the weekend. Of course we were all shocked but the gaffer had done this before with David Kelly, so we thought he must have someone else lined up to replace him. That was arguably the biggest surprise, in that Kevin didn't have a replacement. Apparently the gaffer tried to buy Les Ferdinand but QPR wouldn't sell until the end of the season. There was loads of speculation on who was coming to the club. Roberto Baggio, George Weah and Martin Dahlin were just three. Apparently Baggio was seen at a chippy in Westerhope, Hristo Stoichkov was caught eating a Greggs pasty on Gosforth High Street, while Romario was supposedly drinking Newcastle Brown Ale in Rosie's Bar. It was that type of season.

Paul Kitson was signed earlier that term but I think supporters were disappointed because he didn't score as many goals as Andy. Paul was a different type of player anyway and hadn't been brought in to replace Andy. You always wonder how players would cope coming to a bigger club. Newcastle were growing at a staggering rate and Paul had arrived from a smaller club.

Keith Gillespie was a good addition to the side. He was quick and had a bit of flair. But there were always problems because of his Irish background. He liked a drink and a gamble. He ran up a gambling debt so high that Keegan had to step in and sort it out. The bookies were threatening to go to the papers with the story. The gaffer intervened and told them if they went to the papers they wouldn't get a penny back. It did get out but, from what I believe, the club controlled the story so it wasn't as damaging.

Keith was always telling me funny stories about his drinking adventures and exploits with women. I'm thinking, fucking hell Keith; you need to calm down otherwise you'll find yourself in trouble. He was like, 'Pav, I love the drink and the women.' But he was a young lad, only 19-years-old when he signed for us. You would see him come in for training on some days and he would be stinking of drink. Sometimes he would turn up in the clothes he had worn from the night before; the scruffy bugger. I don't think he fulfilled his full potential because he liked socialising too much. It was a shame. He trained hard though and always gave 100 per cent. He was a lovely lad; wouldn't hurt you in any shape or form.

Ironically, we played Manchester United the weekend after we sold Andy. There was a gentleman's agreement between the two clubs that neither Coley nor Keith would play in that game. The atmosphere was maybe more charged than normal considering the circumstances. But then again the games we had against Man U were always passionate and feisty affairs.

Mark Hughes and I collided as he scored early on and was stretchered off with a knee injury as a consequence. Straight after the game I went to Sir Alex Ferguson and apologised and asked if he would send my best wishes to Mark who had gone straight to the RVI hospital. The following day in training I mentioned to Barry Venison and a couple of the lads that I might go to visit Mark in hospital. Venners told me to leave it and said there was no need. They pointed out, I had already apologised to their manager and it was an accident after all. I wasn't convinced and still wanted to see if he was OK, until Venners said, 'How many times has he fucking knocked you out and never apologised? So there's no need to feel guilty.' Venners was right, of course. Despite that, I still felt responsible. Every time I see him on the TV now, I still think about it. No one wants to see a fellow professional hurt badly. But Mark was one of the toughest opponents I ever faced in my career.

Eric Cantona played in that game but a week or so later he kicked out at a fan at Crystal Palace. The first time I saw Cantona go into the crowd I thought it was a stupid act. But after thinking about it I could understand. It is hard being a stranger in an alien country and the insults foreigners receive is uncalled for. The abuse Eric took that night was probably just once too often and pushed him over the edge. Footballers are under a lot of pressure and there is an enormous amount of tension. I know as professionals we're supposed to keep our composure but you can easily lose it, like Zindine Zidance did when he head butted Marco Materazzi in the 2006 World Cup final. I think, OK, it is fine to insult me, but don't insult or disrespect my family the way Materazzi did with Zidance. I think that is stepping over the line.

Edgar Davids did this to me after a Euro 2000 group game when it was jointly held between Belgium and Holland. We lost 1-0 to a last minute penalty. At the end of the game I was furious about it. As I was coming off the pitch I shouted to a couple of my team mates we were cheated out of winning the game, so they shouldn't shake anyone's hand. As I walked past Denis Berkamp and Davids, Davids shouted, 'Hey, your fucking daughter should die!' I was incensed by this remark and went for him. I screamed, 'I'll smash your fucking glasses.' But when I tried to get at him several players got in the way to prevent me from giving him a good hiding. From that moment on I lost all respect I had for the man and his illustrious career. If I met him in the street now, I would probably smack him one. Maybe I was out of order for telling my colleagues to avoid shaking our opponents' hands. I was livid about an unfair decision, that's all. But did I deserve Davids' insult? He could have told me to fuck off. But to say that to me, I hate the man now.

If I remember rightly it was a bit of a controversial year or season. Paul Merson admitted to taking drugs and having an alcohol problem. I think Tony Adams came out and admitted he had a problem with drinking too. Bruce Grobbelaar was caught on film in some sting about match fixing. One of the games was against us. Andy Cole netted a hat-trick in a 3-0 win at St James' Park. I've seen the goals a few times now and apart from one goal, which you could arguably say, he should've done better, Bruce had no chance. I don't think there was anything untoward. But how many times have people, pundits and the press said 'should've done better' about other goalkeepers. Does that mean we're all doing it?

After finishing third the previous term, expectations were higher than before. We were expected to do even better in the new campaign. We had a stronger squad; we had a Premier League season under our belts and we were quietly confident we could maybe win the league, or at the very least a cup competition. Yet, although we had a good side, that played open attractive football, I was always conscious we didn't have the experience of Manchester United. Even our boss, Kevin Keegan, didn't have the familiarity of Sir Alex Ferguson. He was still a relatively unproven manager despite how well he had sculpted Newcastle into a top Premier League side. But Kevin knew if we were going to progress every year and get closer to Manchester United you had to buy better players and make competition tougher for us each season.

Phillipe Albert and Marc Hottiger were the two major signings brought in before the kick off at Leicester City. They both played for their respective national teams but that was pretty much all I knew about them really. Although if a player arrived at the club with an international pedigree you knew he must be a first-class footballer. Nevertheless, you're always curious to see how the new arrivals respond to the surroundings and wonder whether they will be able to cope with the incredible passion generated by our supporters. It's no place for the feint hearted. And certainly with the foreign players, it seemed there was an unwritten law that they had to be better than their English counterparts. I knew how difficult it was to settle and adjust as a foreign player so I used to try and help out when new lads turned up at St James' Park. Of course the club was better prepared for the foreigners under Keegan, than when I first arrived on Tyneside. The biggest plus, however, was that they could speak English, while I couldn't. It was just by chance that there was someone living in Newcastle from the Czech Republic when I arrived. He approached the club and offered his services as an interpreter. He then helped me settle in, find somewhere to live and translate the language.

Philippe Albert may have been an unusual centre half to most football fans in England but his type were quite common in Europe. You generally have one centre back who can play football, like Philippe, and another like Darren Peacock who could bash it away. Philippe was great at taking people on, good vision, great shot and could score goals, when he wasn't defending. He was a very good footballer.

We started well, unbeaten in 11, nine of them victories, and we were top of the league before tasting our first defeat; a 2-0 loss at Manchester United in late October. Gary Pallister and Keith Gillespie netted. Andy Cole missed the game at Old Trafford through injury. Ironically, we had just beaten the Red Devils 2-0, at home in the League Cup, three days earlier, thanks to late goals from Phillipe Albert and Paul Kitson. However, the two teams were radically different. Sir Alex played about eight of his kids in the cup game. The likes of Paul Scholes, David Beckham, Nicky Butt and the Neville brothers got a run out if I remember correctly. What careers they all went on to have for club and country.

The League Cup was a great night all the same. It was like we had issued a statement of intent. We were more than pretenders to the Manchester United throne. Yet looking back, that's all we really were. After the defeat at Old Trafford we had a difficult spell we never really recovered from. Every team has a sticky patch, whether it is Man United, Chelsea or Liverpool. It is how you recover from a period of playing poorly and get out of it. With Man United it was maybe two or three games; with us it was longer. We only won one game in eight after the defeat in Manchester.

We crashed out of the UEFA Cup to Athletic Bilbao on away goals; won 3-2 at home, lost 1-0 away. We hoped to get the away goal that would take us through to the next stage of the competition but it wasn't to be. The two late goals we conceded in the home leg proved costly to us. We were coasting quite comfortably at 3-0 then the fans were doing a Mexican wave around the stadium and as Kevin said at the time, we got complacent and didn't finish the job. Then there were injuries to several of our key players, notably Barry Venison and Andy Cole, and we lost Phillipe Albert and Scott Sellars for more than half of the season. All of a sudden, our confidence is low and maybe our squad was not as strong as we first thought.

Most of our supporters remember our return to the UEFA Cup with a great deal of fondness. It was the club's first sortie in European competition since 1977 and we got off to a great start in the first round at Royal Antwerp. I know people will look at the 5-0 score and think it was a stroll in the park, but it was anything but that. We scored early on but I had to be at my best, and made four or five saves to keep a clean sheet. It could've easily been 5-5. This was the game where Rob Lee scored a hat-trick and at the end Keegan was on his knees in front of the cameras bowing to our goalscoring midfielder. It was a bit embarrassing. Venners said to me after the game, 'Just forget it, Pav, you were the best player tonight.' It's not that I was looking for any special treatment but a 'well done' would've been nice every now and again.

Rob Lee was a great player for Newcastle and I don't want to take anything away from him. Kevin singled him out for exceptional praise all of the time. I don't think he should've done that because it causes a little resentment. We all used to take the piss out of Rob, saying Kevin was his dad. The gaffer should have spread his praise around all of the players a bit more. Rob was a good player but he didn't do it all by himself. Similarly, at Sparta Prague, at the end of the game, the players always go to the same noisy supporters who sing in the corner. They should really go and appreciate all the fans and not just those who make the most noise.

I started the season as the club's number one goalkeeper but it was always in the back of my mind Kevin would bring in someone else after it didn't work out with Mike Hooper. Why did I think that? I thought that because Keegan always did it. Last season he bought Mike and this term was no different. He tried to sign the USA international Brad Freidel.

There were several times in the past where one of the lads would open a newspaper at training and read that we were linked with a keeper. Understandably, they would take the piss. That is part and parcel of being in a dressing room. It would be something like, 'Hey, Pav, I see someone else is after your shirt,' or, 'I see you have another friend coming to keep you company.' But that happened with all the players. Alan Shearer was always winding up the lads with stuff like this; although he wasn't there at this time. I remember when we had the Entertainers' exhibition game against Liverpool at Kingston Park when we had all retired. One of the Liverpool players chipped me to score. After the match Shearer came into the dressing room and said, 'Some things never fucking change, eh, Pav?' But that was Alan, he always had a wisecrack for the occasion. I just laughed.

Brad came to train with us midway through this season. He was a good goalkeeper and was with us for a couple of months. But he couldn't get a work permit at the time because he didn't meet the criteria needed.

At the time you had to have played in 75 per cent of the games for your national team.

The team all went out for a drink down the Quayside one evening when Brad was training with us. Later on, the pair of us headed back up home; and he said that I was the best goalkeeper he had trained with at the time. I returned the compliment because, to be fair, Brad was good. I have met a few people from the USA in my lifetime and the majority of them have been loud, crass and had an unswerving belief that they are the best thing since the wheel was invented. I have to say I never experienced any of that with Brad. We never had a problem with each other. I never fell out with any goalkeeper during my time at Newcastle. Had Brad managed to get a work permit, however, I knew he would've replaced me as the club's number one. In fact I told him that. He acknowledged what I had said and recognised that I would be a tough challenger for the number one shirt.

I think Kevin would've been happy for me to be a number two, where he could maybe call on me two or three times a season, but I wasn't happy with that. I suppose when you think of Mike Hooper, he was in a worse position than I was because I had replaced him in the pecking order. If another keeper came in he would be the club's third choice. Mike even said that to me in the dressing room one day: 'Pav, looks like I'm finished here now.'

Every game I felt under enormous pressure because I thought if I make a mistake, then I would be out of the team. I got a lot of help from the players. They were always very supportive towards me in times like this but obviously they don't pick the team. Darren

Peacock, for example, was great with me. Yes, he would shout and scream, but it wasn't personal. It was only because he wanted to win. This encouragement to never give up kept me going if I'm honest. They believed in me and this was a massive boost to my confidence. I often say this to my goalkeepers now at Sparta Prague, that when they are feeling low, they will get support from the players.

When we were going through our bad spell Kevin never lost his temper the way he did after the match at Leeds when we were going for the title. But there was one match where we played poorly and he had us in for training on the Sunday, which he'd never done before. Usually after a match we would get the next day off. He even had us goalkeepers training with players, when in the past we would work out our sessions alone. Maybe this was tougher for Kevin than it was for us. If you remember he had always played for successful teams that won trophies, such as Liverpool and Hamburg. He probably hadn't experienced anything like this before and was struggling to find inspiration. He had Terry McDermott with him but he did nothing. Terry Mac would lean on the post and watch the sessions in training. He wouldn't get involved. Players would take the piss out of him. They'd say, 'Watch out, Terry,' and he would reply, 'It's OK, Pav will save it.' I would love to get an assistant manager's job like Terry had. He did fuck all and got very well paid for it. Derek Fazackerley did just about everything on the training pitch. Terry was Kevin's friend, that was about it.

While our form in the league was faltering, we still fancied ourselves to win the FA Cup. We could beat anyone on our day. We were handed a tough home draw in the third round against Alan Shearer's Blackburn. It didn't look good when they managed to get a draw and take us back to Ewood Park. Even worse, Pedro was injured for the replay. Yet we managed to beat them 2-1 thanks to a late Lee Clark goal after Chris Sutton cancelled out Mark Hottiger's opener. It was a great result considering Rovers won the league that year.

Paul Kitson bagged a hat-trick as we saw off Swansea at St James' Park in the fourth round before we despatched Manchester City, 3-1, in yet another home tie. Keith Gillespie grabbed a brace and Bez netted the other. We travelled to Everton in the sixth round as favourites but ended up losing to a scruffy Dave Watson goal. Everton were a tough, physical side, while we liked to get it down and play. It was a horrible game to play in. We just didn't get the rub of the green in that match in the same way we didn't get it against Bilbao in the UEFA Cup.

Obviously we were disappointed to go out of the FA Cup but we still had things to play for. We were third in the league. The title was out of our reach because Blackburn and Man U were too far ahead, although we could still qualify for the UEFA Cup. A spectacular Peter Beardsley goal against Arsenal in injury time gave us three valuable points, after the Everton defeat, but we couldn't quite build on it. We subsequently won only two and drew three out of our last nine games. Why did we collapse? The injuries to key players didn't help. But maybe there was a lack of belief and confidence in the camp. Whatever it was we couldn't put another consistent run together like we did at the beginning of the new season.

It could have been the second season syndrome, where teams were a little bit more wise to us, while we struggled to adjust to teams finding us out. We finished sixth that season, which wasn't too bad when you think about it; but we didn't qualify for Europe. That was disappointing. European competition was special for everyone. We had a taste of it and wanted more but it wasn't to be that year. But after the way we started the season it definitely felt like a failure.

We were top of the league until mid November and then gradually lost ground. I think there were a couple of games towards the end of the season which kind of typified our campaign. The home fixture against Spurs was one of those games. We took a 2-0 lead within ten minutes but then the game turned on its head and we were 3-2 down after less than half an hour. I got sent off for bringing down either Nick Barmby or Jurgen Klinsman, I can't quite remember who it was because it happened so fast. Mike Hooper came on and saved the penalty and then Pedro equalised later on. I asked Kevin and Russell Cushing to appeal against it because I shouldn't have been sent off. I remember Russell telling me if he appealed and it failed I would get an extra match ban. It was a case of damned if you don't, damned if you do. It cost me my place in the team for the start of the 1995-96 season because I was suspended. I was disappointed with the club because I felt they didn't do enough with the appeal. And it probably gave Kevin an excuse to bring in another goalkeeper. Not that he needed one. I know that sounds petty but it was how I was feeling at the time.

A few days before the North-East Player of the Year Awards, Venners asked me to find out from the boss who had won, when we were coming back from an away match. Keegan wouldn't tell him, you see. When I asked the gaffer he started laughing and said: 'You think you have a chance, Pav?' I said no, but Venners and I would like to know.

Keegan reckoned he didn't know but I think he did. I thought I was in with a chance because Venners had missed more than 20 games that season, and it is harder to keep that high standard of play. When Venners won it, I thought it was a little strange because I was sure I was the best player that year. Even Peter Beardsley thought so. He told me at the awards ceremony: 'It's not right you didn't win the trophy.' I think maybe Pedro knew something about it and was trying to tell me that this was the way things worked. Whatever, it was a terrible disappointment for me. But I have to say Venners was fantastic that season. Kevin had switched Barry to the centre of midfield anchor role, with the arrival of Marc Hottiger at right back, and won two England caps in that position. He didn't look out of place in the Three Lions' line up and played well in both games.

It wasn't a great season for the team but I was reasonably happy because I had played every game with the exception of those fixtures when I was suspended. Barry Venison and I probably had our best campaigns for Newcastle in the 1994-95 season. I had established myself as the club's number one shot stopper. Yet I knew I was going to be suspended for start of the new season and once again, wondered who Kevin was going to bring in to replace me.

CHAPTER 8
SECOND BEST

It may have been christened the greatest Premier League match of all time, but for me it was the worst moment and memory of my entire career. Losing the Euro 1996 final to Germany was a tough experience but I wasn't between the posts for that game. I wouldn't care, I used to love going to Anfield. My first game for the reserves was at Liverpool and I performed magnificently. I always seemed to have a good game when I visited the red side of Merseyside so I was really looking forward to the contest. Kevin was going around the dressing room prior to the kick off, having the odd word of encouragement with some of the players. Admittedly, we'd had a mixed bag of results before this fixture but we were still confident of winning. Then, just before we went out onto the pitch, Keegan turned to me and said, 'Pav, why can't you be more like Schmeichel, and win a game for us?'

I was astounded! Those words killed me! I was deflated! After he said that, I couldn't play. I felt as if I'd just been smashed on the head. Anything I'd been feeling prior to that comment: adrenaline, excitement and anticipation, all of the emotions you generally experience before you run onto the pitch prior to a match, had evaporated! I had nothing! No strength; no confidence; no will; nothing. Keegan might as well have said, 'You're shit! I have no faith in you.' I was thinking, I can't go and play now. I need to tell him. But then I thought I have to go and play. My head was all over the place. I couldn't concentrate on the game. I resented Kevin at that point. This was one of the biggest games of the season. And he'd more or less told me I was a second rate goalkeeper. I had never been given any words of encouragement in all of my time at the club. I thought what have you ever done for me? Every time he knocked me on the floor, one way or another, I had to pick myself up, dust myself down and get on with it.

Were any of the goals my fault? Maybe one of them was down to me; perhaps one of the Collymore goals. I just tried to spread myself the best I could. But I wasn't mentally right during the game. The last words Kevin said to me just kept going around and around in my head all the way through the game. Losing the match, conceding the goals and in essence throwing away the title; they weren't the worst things for me. It was Keegan's words prior to going out to play; they were a hammer blow. I have never watched a replay or any highlights of that game because it is too painful a memory. I can still hear Kevin saying those hurtful words now. It makes me sad. I don't know whether the score would've been any different and the course of history would've been changed. But I would've been up for the game more. I have never discussed this with anyone before. It's been a burden I've carried around with me ever since that fateful night.

After the game we were all disconsolate. The dressing room was like a morgue and we were all zombies, walking dead. We knew the title was slowly slipping through our fingers. It was drifting away. I can't remember Kevin coming into the dressing room after the match and giving any words of encouragement. He might have done but not to my memory. I think he was just as devastated as we were. Arthur Cox was always the man who tried to lift the team, anyway, not Kevin or Terry Mac. It wouldn't have mattered because no words could have eased any pain I was feeling at that point.

Game after game came our way and more tension and pressure continued to build up. I was dropped after the Liverpool match and Shaka was back in. Shaka never offered any words of encouragement nor did any of the other players. We were all down. We were all feeling sorry for ourselves. At the same time when Shaka played poorly I never said anything to him. It's fair to say I thought I was finished at Newcastle after the game at Anfield. I believed I'd played my last match and my career was over on Tyneside.

Kevin Keegan wasn't the only high profile manager, personality or pundit who did not rate me as a goalkeeper. I remember Bob Wilson offering his opinion in a newspaper article prior to the 1995-96 season. In it he wrote off Newcastle's chances of winning the Premier League because, in the former Arsenal and Scotland shot stopper's opinion, you couldn't win a title without a decent goalkeeper. In essence, he was saying I wasn't good enough.

You often wonder why people, such as Wilson, are asked to give an opinion about a club or player when they have absolutely no connection with it. What was his motive? Had someone asked Ronnie Simpson, Willie McFaul or Mick Mahoney, then fair enough. They had a relationship, link or association with Newcastle. Wilson did not; he played all of his football in London with Arsenal. I felt something wasn't quite right and maybe there was a bit of a conspiracy going on. Sure enough, I later find out Wilson is Shaka Hislop's coach at Reading. It seemed he was pushing up the profile of his protégé.

The last thing I want is to be disrespectful or criticise Shaka because he became a friend of mine and was a good keeper. What I am trying to say, had Keegan brought in a World Class goalkeeper who was better than me, then I would hold my hands up and say, 'OK, he is better than me!' But he didn't do that. At that time I didn't know what supporters, players or critics thought until later. In time, I soon found out everyone felt the same as I did. That yes, Kevin signed a few good goalkeepers but none of them were better than I was. The best goalkeeper I played and trained with was Petr Koba, the Czech Republic number one. I probably would have claimed 100 caps for my country had he not been around. So I can admit there were better goalkeepers out there than I was.

I remember the pictures of Shaka and Kevin together and how the press made out he was one in a million, in that he was earning £1m a year. Obviously, discovering that made me feel great, being the club's poor pauper on £150,000 a year. I didn't read the newspapers because one: Ossie Ardiles told me not too, and two, despite my English improving, it was still difficult to understand what was written in them. But I always got the information somehow, whether it was one of the lads in the team or my friend Denis Martin. I knew that my days were numbered. You don't pay £1.5m for a goalkeeper just for him to sit on the bench.

At the time there were a lot of former goalkeepers, such as Peter Shilton and Bob Wilson, saying there were too many foreign keepers in the country. My response would always be, the British keepers should play better to get a place in the team, or ask why clubs are buying foreign players? I'll tell you why, because they are cheaper and better. There was always an argument that foreign keepers didn't come out for crosses. But neither did our British counterparts. Peter Shilton never came for crosses and neither did Shay Given, and look at what fantastic careers they both had.

A lot of critics, writers and the pundits were, also, falling over themselves to make comments about us. And the observations were generally negative, despite the open, attractive and exciting football we played. They seemed to resent us. I don't know why. Maybe it was because we were upsetting the old football guard or hierarchy such as Liverpool and Arsenal. On *Match of the Day*, there were many a time when, ex Liverpool defender, Alan Hansen absolutely slaughtered us. He seemed to take great pleasure pointing out weaknesses in our set up or how to beat us. Why did he do it? I do not know. Maybe he didn't like us or some of our personnel or that we were doing better than his beloved Liverpool. Maybe it was because it wasn't the way he was brought up to play or liked to play. I know that if pundits, writers or critics were having a go at him, he wouldn't like it, yet there he was, hammering us, criticising and in general being destructive.

Nevertheless, another new season was upon us and there was fresh optimism, which, to be honest, was always the case every time we returned for preseason. We were installed as the Premier League favourites despite our meltdown in the second half of the last campaign. The gaffer went out shopping in the summer and spent £6m on Les Ferdinand, £4m on Warren Barton, £2.5m on David Ginola and, of course, £1.5m on Shaka. I was no different to the rest of our supporters. I was excited at the prospect of seeing them all in action.

I played against Les when he was at QPR and he always seemed to do well against us. It was no surprise when we signed him. The newspapers were full of his imminent arrival on Tyneside. We knew what a good player he was, but the former QPR striker surprised us even more in training on his first day. Some of the lads were banging in crosses for Les. And he was leaping about five yards off the ground and hanging in fresh air. I was standing watching this with Keegan, Terry Mac and some of the lads and it was incredible. It was unbelievable how high he could get up to head the ball. He was also such a powerfully strong man. I thought, what a buy he is going to be if he can produce this on a Saturday afternoon.

But football ability aside, Les was a fantastic man. I would love to have stolen some fashion tips from him but I couldn't afford the clothes he bought. He always looked smart, dressed well and he was popular with the ladies. And he wasn't called Big Les for nothing. I remember one day, he was towelling himself down after he had come out of the shower and his crown jewels were on show.

The gaffer said, 'Les, I don't want any of your money, your houses or your riches. I want to borrow that, just for an hour. I'll visit my wife and then you can have it back.' The comment had all of the lads in hysterics.

Les was subject to a newspaper sting when he was at Newcastle. He had been set up by a tabloid newspaper. A photographer was waiting to take pictures of him with a woman. I can't remember where, but it happened. I recall Keegan got involved and tried to keep it out of the papers. Kevin was always good with stuff like that. There were a few lads in my time at Newcastle who had off the field problems, such as Keith Gillespie and Barry Venison. But it was the exception rather than the rule. In general we had a squeaky clean bunch of professionals. All of the lads knew about the newspaper set up. There is no doubt Les' form dipped after Christmas but, he wasn't the only one. Whether it was connected to this I do not know.

Unlike Les, we didn't know much about David Ginola when he first arrived on Tyneside. I remember a few players being put out when the sponsored cars were being handed out at the beginning of the season. We all got a Rover while Ginola got a big Range Rover. I remember Rob Lee taking the piss out of him, saying, 'Ah, you must be something special, eh? And we're shit because you get the big car and we don't.' I know Rob was having a laugh with David but there were some players pissed off about it.

I thought David was a great guy with an overwhelming amount of charisma. You don't get all of this special treatment if you didn't have an exceptional talent. After I saw him in action, however, I realised that maybe he was worth all of the fuss. Later on we heard about why he left France and how a mistake he made cost France going to the World Cup in 1994. It's outrageous he was blamed for Les Bleus' exit from the competition. I later saw a replay of the incident on TV. Ginola lost the ball in the corner of the opposition's half. It wasn't as if he had left a back pass too short; scored an own goal or hadn't tracked his man back. But it seemed as if the whole country were against him. The press, supporters and even his manager at the time, Gerard Houllier, blamed David. Little wonder he wanted to escape France.

David was extremely intelligent and very knowledgeable about music and fashion. I used to love listening to him talk about music, whether it was jazz, rock or pop. He was really passionate about the subject. He was a fascinating man as well as a fantastic footballer. He had flair on the pitch and was just as flamboyant off it. Even now he still has elegance, style and good taste. He lived in St Tropez, where his house was built into a rock. He lived in a different world to the majority of us, a very luxurious lifestyle. He was also a very good rally driver. David became a target for Newcastle supporters when he left after he made one or two disagreeable comments about the club. But I know he loved his short time on Tyneside. Ginola told me that he expected to end his football career at St James' Park. Newcastle fans have Kenny Dalglish to thank for that. He also shared his plans to become a rally driver at the end of his career. Renault had offered him a remarkable contract to drive for them with better money than he earned from playing football. I'm not sure whether he took up that offer but he did go on to become an actor.

In the first six months of his time with us I never saw anything better. He was amazing. Then, for some reason or other, people got on his back because he never tracked defenders back in. This followed Ginola throughout his career. People thought he was lazy, but that was his style of football. And in most of his time with us he never chased back either. It was only when we had a dip in form and started losing games it became an issue. Ginola had an argument with Shearer about it in the dressing room the following year.

I was suspended for the first three matches of the season thanks to a sending off in the home fixture with Tottenham. I didn't get back in the team until December when we played Chelsea away in the league. I came on for Shaka who got a thigh injury during the game. But my season was turned around when we played Everton at home in the following fixture. I wouldn't care; I'd played for the reserves at Everton the week before and had a nightmare, conceding five goals in the process. Yet I arguably had the game of my life in the hard-fought contest at St James' Park. We won 1-0 thanks to a Les Ferdinand strike.

We were up against it for most of the game because Bez was sent off after only half an hour for a professional foul on Andrei Kanchelskis. I had most of my friends and family over the game as well which made the match extra special. But the pièce de résistance came when I changed direction in mid flight to tip over an Anders Limpar deflected shot off Steve Howey. I was very proud to hear England goalkeeping legend Gordon Banks say it was in his top ten saves of all time. He was one of the greatest goalkeepers that ever lived, so when a man of his reputation says something like that, it must mean something. I got a standing ovation at the end of the game. It was an emotional moment for me and my family, who were crying because of this outpour of love and affection from the supporters. This happened a few times at Newcastle and I couldn't even start to explain how this made me feel and what it meant to me. Their appreciation more than evened out all of the bad times I had suffered at the club.

I didn't have much to cheer about up until that point of the season. The team were doing well but when you're not involved you feel left out. I kept myself going by getting my head down in training and working hard, which I really enjoyed. But that is all I had at the time. Being excluded from the first team picture affects your personal life. My wife often said, she would never marry another footballer because I was walking around like a miserable bastard when I wasn't playing. It put her under a lot of stress. This got even worse when I was playing for the Czech Republic later in my career. People would stop and stare at her in the street because they knew she was my wife and they blamed me for a World Cup qualifying defeat. It made her feel guilty and she hadn't done anything.

We were still fighting on three fronts for the league, League Cup and FA Cup as we entered the second week of January. But within a fortnight we only had the Premier League title to focus our attentions on. After a hard-fought draw at Stamford Bridge in the FA Cup third round, we travelled to Highbury to play Arsenal in the fifth round of the League Cup. We had just beaten the Gunners in the league a week before the contest and were confident of turning them over on their home patch.

Ian Wright gave the hosts a lead a minute before the break. Kevin actually criticised me on television for conceding the first goal after the match had finished but the ball swerved in front of me. We actually had a few words about it in the dressing room at half time. Even if you watch the highlights now you'll hear Martin Tyler and Ron Atkinson commentating on how the ball had viciously swerved three times as it went past me. I remember Ian Wright was interviewed after the game on TV and pointed out that I had no chance because the ball had swerved. I was thankful to Wrighty but Keegan still blamed me all the same. The referee didn't have a good game that night. Some of the tackles were X-rated and Ginola was getting kicked from pillar to post by Lee Dixon and then Nigel Winterburn. The Frenchman eventually snapped, elbowing Dixon in the face. He got a red card. The game was highly charged and spilled over into the dugouts where Arsenal boss Bruce Rioch and Terry Mac squared up with each other. It was a disappointment to lose the game because it was a trophy we felt we could win.

We then crashed out of the FA Cup in the third round. We managed to draw 1-1 at Chelsea but lost the replay on penalties after it finished level, 2-2, after extra time. I think we were unlucky in both games because we were the better side but didn't get much luck. We could now concentrate on the league. Or rather that was what we felt.

There was a lot of tension and pressure on us prior to the visit of Man United. I think we were six points clear of them before they arrived on Tyneside. That aside, we had a great team and were still confident of beating them. And anyone who saw the game will tell you, we absolutely battered them, but couldn't score. We had several chances and Peter Schmeichel made four or five outstanding saves and they scored a goal from a counterattack. The ball came from right to left and found Eric Cantona at the back post. He hit it into the ground and across me to score. It was a proper smash and grab result because we murdered them on the night. People say the Liverpool result was the catalyst for our destruction that season. But had we beat Man U on that occasion we would have put nine points between us. Even a draw would've been a good result. Our lead was cut to three points after that game.

Peter Schmeichel developed his own style over the years and opened up another approach to goalkeeping. He was quite unconventional in technique I suppose. He was a big man who spread himself out and it wouldn't matter what part of the body it hit, as long as he kept the ball out. It wasn't pretty at times but it was effective. I don't think we'll ever see his likes again. He was a one off. He was lucky to have had such a great team in front of him and was very well protected by two experienced centre halves in Steve Bruce and Gary Pallister.

Peter and I weren't great friends but we had mutual respect for one another. Schmeichel approached me once after a game one time, in the lounge, after we lost a game at Old Trafford. He told me not to worry, that I would find another club because I was a good goalkeeper. He must have been aware of my situation, where I was in and out of the side, I guess. It was nice of him to say something. Maybe there was a bit of solidarity between us because we both arrived in

England in 1991 and, being foreigners, had a tough time settling in.

It goes without saying I was down after the defeat at Liverpool and found it hard to get motivated in training. I wasn't the only one. The mood in training was low and almost sombre during this mid slump. The upbeat bouncy nature of training had changed. I didn't look forward to training around this time. It had lost its sparkle. I think it was because we didn't know how to cope. We weren't an experienced side in the same way Man United were. Only Peter Beardsley, and later David Batty, had won a title. It was as if we were looking around for guidance but there was none there. We needed a leader or a strong personality at the back who would say, 'Right, we've gone 1-0 up, now everybody get back behind the ball and defend it.' Pedro was our captain, but he played up front. This was maybe one of Keegan's weaknesses, building a team from the front rather than the back. We never changed our system at all, throughout this period. It was 100 miles an hour all of the time. That was what we were used too and encouraged to play. But saying that, we only conceded two more than Man U that season, but they scored about 15 more.

We beat QPR 2-1 three days after the defeat on Merseyside before losing by the odd goal in three at Blackburn. Shaka was back in goal in place of me and, he would probably tell you, he didn't play well in those games. Generally when either Shaka or I played poorly, we would be out and there would be a change of goalkeeper. This never helped the side, I'm convinced of it. But Kevin always built his team from the top and not the bottom. For me, the goalkeeper is the most important player. If you keep a clean sheet you won't lose the game. I know people will say but you're a goalkeeper Pav, you would say that. That is fair enough but if you look at the game today I bet the goalkeeper is one of the best paid players in the team. When I played the goalkeepers were the worst paid. Why has that changed? Managers or coaches have finally realised that it is a key position in the team. It is the base of the spine.

We managed to string together three 1-0 victories against Aston Villa, Southampton and Leeds United. We were still fighting for the title but the shoe was very much on the other foot now and we were chasing Manchester United. We were all on the bus waiting to travel back to Newcastle when we heard about Keegan's 'I would love it' outburst after the game at Elland Road. One of the lads, I can't remember who, said, 'Keegan has just lost it on the TV,' but no one saw until later that night when we got home or the following day. There was a TV on the bus but it wasn't on.

How did the players feel about his explosion? We all thought he was right to hold Ferguson to account for comments he made about the commitment of Leeds, and later Nottingham Forest, players. We had already agreed to play in a testimonial for Forest legend Stuart Pearce, the previous term. But we had to visit the County Ground to play Forest in the penultimate game of the season. Of course Kevin should've have been more composed but emotions were running high. It was out of character and unlike him. Generally the gaffer was calmness personified. But there's no getting away from the fact that Ferguson was out of order. Some were saying he was playing mind games but many others, including us, disagreed. The Man United boss was taking gamesmanship to another level. He was questioning the integrity and professionalism of Leeds United and Nottingham Forest players. He was out of order and way out of line.

We drew our final two games of the season: 1-1 at Forest and 1-1 at home to Spurs. Even if we had won both of them we would have lost the title on goal difference. The Red Devils had a better goal difference of nine goals.

To this day people are still speculating to why or how we let slip a 12 point lead and lose the title. There wasn't one single reason why we lost the title. There are several explanations why it slipped through our fingers. We had a slump in form which coincided with Man United having a turnaround in fortunes. Maybe we shouldn't have changed our goalkeepers as often as we did. Maybe our manager wasn't tactically as good as other bosses in the Premier League. We could ask the 36,000 supporters, who turned up to watch us, week in and week out, why we lost the title. I bet they would all say something different. Tino and David Batty were blamed. Whatever, the buck stops with the manager. If things go well, the manager gets the praise. If things go wrong, the manager gets the blame.

The board could have said we've given you £60m to spend, why haven't you delivered some silverware? Or maybe the board didn't sign the players Kevin wanted and we were still a couple of players short of winning the title. Maybe the chairman says look we've bought Ferdinand, Ginola, Barton, Hislop and then

Asprilla and Batty, that should be enough. We don't know. Maybe we had too many individual flair players whereas Man United had more of a team. So it's all hypothetical why we didn't win the league. There is one player I think could've helped land our first top flight title since 1927, but we let him go. You'll find out who I am referring too if you turn to the chapter on my greatest Newcastle United team.

The media, pundits and writers had a lot to say about us that season. How we should be doing this and that, and we will never win the league if we didn't do this and that. I think Kevin was influenced by this. He was told he couldn't win the league without a new goalkeeper. Next thing that happens, Shaka Hislop arrives. We are told we need a defensive midfielder and then David Batty turns up at St James' Park. We're not scoring enough goals, and then Faustino Asprilla is signed. What happens next? We throw away the title.

Batty was a hard man on the pitch. It was an unusual signing because Batty was a defensive midfield player yet Kevin still wanted us to play the same way. So you could say he upset the rhythm of the side, through no fault of his own.

The difference between coaching now and back then at Newcastle couldn't be any more different. Now it is all planning, tactics and watching videos. Back then we never had one meeting, one video or one talk. Kevin would chuck a ball at us and tell us to go and play. Admittedly, I think the game is over complicated now, yet there were times I felt Kevin could've changed the game by being more tactically astute with his substitutions; the formation and shape

I remember going out onto the pitch on the last day of the season to salute those magnificent supporters after we drew with Spurs for the customary lap of honour. It was heartbreaking. We were all distraught. Darren Peacock was crying and there were tears in the eyes of several others. We didn't know what the future held I suppose. We were thinking was the team going to be broken up? Every season I had been at the club, up to that point, was generally finished on a high. This was our best season ever, yet it felt the worst. Had we won the title it would have changed everyone's life for the better, forever. You get more respect around the world for being a champion. You would get better contracts and more money. We missed out on so much. They probably would have built statues of us all at St James' Park.

I know this time, era, is cherished in the memory of every Newcastle United fan. There was something special about the period; something intangible enveloping the city, yet at the same time you could almost touch it. Music, culture and politics were changing and we were part of that zeitgeist. I am aware that we are still loved and cherished for the carefree, swashbuckling way we played our football. I know supporters were excited before a game and got an enormous amount pleasure out of our time there. But we failed to deliver any silverware and it hurts deeply. There isn't a day that goes by without thinking about what could've been had we delivered that trophy to those loyal supporters.

CHAPTER 9
FROM TYNE TO WEAR?

Kevin Keegan quitting was a massive bombshell. The players heard the gaffer had tendered his resignation to Sir John Hall at the end of the previous season for failing to land the Premier League title. But the United owner rejected the offer and persuaded Kevin to stop on. We still didn't expect him to walk out but then maybe we should have seen it coming. We had gone seven league games without a win and it all seemed to culminate after the match at Ewood Park on Boxing Day. It was the only time I'd seen Keegan lose his temper.

It all kicked off in the dressing room after the 1-0 defeat. The gaffer tore a strip off a few players, Les Ferdinand in particular, who had gone two months without scoring a goal. He told Les he wasn't worth the wages the club were paying him after his performance that day. The gaffer's attack really upset Les, so much so that he slapped in a transfer request. The argument was relatively heated. Les countered Keegan's charge by saying the club had given him his contract, not Kevin. Rob Lee was another player who was upset by Kevin's volley. I'm not saying the boss lost the dressing room after this incident but he certainly lost a lot of respect from the players. The scenario was uncomfortable viewing for all of the squad there, not just those involved. Did Kevin think he couldn't motivate or take the team any further at this point? Maybe this was true, we were having a wretched run of form up to that moment in time and couldn't buy a win from anywhere.

I remained first choice up until that reversal at Blackburn. The Blackburn episode turned out to be a watershed moment for the direction of club because Kevin offered to resign after our lacklustre defeat to Rovers. Nevertheless, Keegan was still in charge for the visit of Tottenham two days later. And he named the team for the home clash in his office. Surprise surprise, Shaka was back in nets. We're struggling to score goals yet he changes the goalkeeper.

I waited for everyone to leave the office before I asked Keegan why Shaka was being preferred to me. He didn't have an answer at first. He seemed too preoccupied to respond. But I kept on at him, asking, 'Give me one reason. Was my performance not good enough? Why?' You could see he wasn't happy with me but in the end he said, 'He can kick the ball further than you.' I thanked him and left his office. I think this response would've said more to him than had I kicked off and had a blazing row. I could've asked if he was sure Shaka could kick it further than me, but what would be the point?

Before the game I went to see my friend, Roy Hutchinson, and told him the tale. He couldn't believe it. We beat Spurs 7-1, probably because of Shaka's kicking. I knew it was a stupid answer from Kevin, and he only said it to get rid of me. But I wanted some sort of explanation because I was sick and tired of being in and out of the side. It pissed me off. Before this I had never banged on Kevin's door demanding an answer to why I was dropped. I usually just accepted it. But this time I hadn't done anything wrong so I demanded an answer. Within a week of this Keegan had resigned.

There was no clue or hint that Kevin was going to leave, quit or whether he got pushed. You could never really measure whether he was happy or unhappy because his demeanour or body language was always the same. But to be honest, I wasn't interested in whether he was happy, sad or indifferent. I was pissed off with Kevin. I was thinking more about my situation than anyone else's problems. That aside, when the dust settled, we were all upset with Kevin when he quit. He never came to say goodbye to any one of us. And when you think of the five years we had just been through, I think he owed us at least a goodbye. Even a week or so after he left, we still thought he would turn up and see us and tell us why it hadn't worked out.

Keegan had gone and I was thinking of doing the same. I'd had enough. I couldn't take anymore of the yo-yoing in and out of the team so I went to see Arthur Cox and told him I wanted to move. Arthur listened to what I had to say and was very understanding and acknowledged my circumstances. But he asked if I could wait and show some patience. Arthur promised he would take care of my situation if I promised not to do anything impetuous, like put in a transfer request. I gave my word I wouldn't. But, when I found out I wasn't in the starting XI for the Aston Villa match, I was furious.

I deliberated for a while but then thought, no, I'm not waiting any longer. I've had enough of this. I'd had six years of being in and out of the side. I was angry and frustrated. It was the straw that broke the camel's back, so I went to Russell Cushing's office and put in a transfer request. I'm thinking Keegan is not here now and I'm still not getting a game. I thought Arthur would have selected me for the fixture at Villa Park. It certainly looked that way when we had our chat. I let my emotions get the better of me. I know my behaviour upset Arthur and I don't think he has ever forgiven me for this. I have never really apologised to him for my actions, so if you're reading this, Arthur, I'm sorry. I should've waited. I think it was the only time in my life that I broke my word.

When I put in my transfer request I got a call from Peter Reid. I don't know how he got my number or who gave it to him. Apparently when you make a request all clubs in the Premier League and Football League are alerted to your availability. I don't know whether this was the case or whether the story of my request was leaked out. Peter didn't call Newcastle, as far as I'm aware, he just rang my home number. He had a house in Sunderland, somewhere, so I went to see him. We had a friendly chat and he told me he rated me as a keeper and tried to sign me before but was refused permission to talk to me. The Black Cats boss explained how he wanted to build a new side and wanted me to be part of it. He said there was no pressure and that I should go away and think about it. I seriously thought about the move. From a family point of view it would've been convenient because I wouldn't have to move and could still send my daughter to the same school.

The news got out in the press and fans were stopping me in the street asking if there was any truth in the rumour. The reaction was mixed. There were a lot of fans who could understand my dilemma, of not being a regular goalkeeper, so they wished me luck. The other half were pleading with me not to go because it would break their hearts while some said they would hate me. I used to have this little Cocker Spaniel dog and I would walk him every day in a field, near St Nicholas' Hospital in Gosforth. One old man I met said, 'You've put up with a lot of shit here, Pav, you should go and kick start your career again. I am a Geordie lad and support Newcastle but you should go.' I understood both sides of the argument. It would've been a new challenge for me yet at the same time I didn't want to sour the relationship I had with the Geordie public.

I understood the feeling, passion and hatred between the two sets of fans, cities and clubs. I saw that when Lee Clark left for the Stadium of Light. I also heard from the likes of Barry Venison and Paul Bracewell, who had both played for the Mackems. I also played in a few North-East derbies so I got a taste of the bitterness. But being a foreigner, I didn't hate or dislike Sunderland. I knew what it meant. It was the same when I played for Brescia against Atlanta in Bergamo. The opposition fans put out our team coach windows. We were 3-0 down, I remember, and Roberto Baggio came off the bench to score a hat-trick. It was an amazing match. I recently had friends over for a Sparta Prague versus Slavia Prague derby and they don't hate Slavia, in the same way I don't hate Sunderland. I understand it, though.

The chat I had with Peter Reid was just before the end of the old transfer window. I remember taking my mobile phone and slipping it into my kitbag, on to the training ground. Every 20 minutes or so I would have a look just to see whether there had been any calls. Some of the lads got wind of what was happening and started taking the piss. They were shouting, 'Pav, you never usually bring your kit bag onto the training ground,' and, 'Why you checking your phone every five minutes?' and, 'Any transfer news yet, Pav?' They knew I wasn't happy but it was all good natured banter. I don't know whether Peter got in touch with the club or not or whether he went through the correct channels and the club denied him the chance to talk to me. In the end I didn't have to make the choice because I didn't hear anything else from him.

We went back for preseason in 1996 and it felt a little different. It felt like something had died. Maybe we were all emotionally and psychologically scarred from last term's exploits. You obviously hope you can improve on the previous campaign. That was the aim every year, to get better and better. But as soon as we had a couple of bad results the memories of last season came flooding back and doubt set in. It was still fresh in the memory.

There were loads of rumours and speculation about us signing Alan Shearer, just as we were about to go on tour to Thailand, Singapore and Japan. But once we got on the plane to the Far East we were largely cut off from any media frenzy. We were totally oblivious to the signing of our new £15m striker. We didn't know anything about it until he turned up in Thailand for training.

We were already out on the training pitch going through our warm up and stretching exercises. We were lying on the ground and couldn't see anything. All of a sudden we heard this crunch, crunch, crunch and thud, thud, thud noise on the grass. We looked up and couldn't see anything for what seemed like hundreds of photographers. Then all of a sudden there was a parting in a sea of snappers and out ran Alan. It was surreal. The media wasn't as fast back in those days so we were completely in the dark. Then the gaffer said, 'Boys, this is Alan Shearer.' We were like, fucking hell! We couldn't believe it. We had signed one of the world's best strikers; top goal scorer from Euro 96 and the Premier League. It was totally unexpected. Everyone was excited by his signing. It not only captured the imagination of the supporters, public and media, but us players as well.

Obviously I had played against Alan a few times when he was at Blackburn. He was strong and tough and he caught me in the face with his studs once when I was diving. It was a 50/50 ball and it wasn't intentional. It didn't stop it hurting mind. When he got his body in-between the ball and the player, a raging rhinoceros couldn't take him out. I previously mentioned that our defensive record was as good as Man United's the previous season. The only difference was that we didn't score enough goals. With Alan signing, he had the extra 15 to 20 goals missing from the side that finished runners up.

I know Les wasn't very happy about Alan taking the number nine shirt off him but there was never a problem between the two of them. They became great friends. Alan was the club's biggest capture, the most expensive signing in the world at the time, and would've got anything he asked for. There were a lot of dissenters saying Alan and Les were both target men and wouldn't be able to play together but they proved them wrong. They were both perfect foil for one another. Not a lot of people know this but Ferdinand was only behind Nobby Solano and Laurent Robert in providing the most assists for Shearer throughout his Newcastle career, and he only played one season with him at St James' Park. Many of Shearer's goals came courtesy of the second ball. Les would get up and win the first one from a corner, or set play, and Alan was always on hand to bang it in.

Alan was a big personality and a strong character. He was a funny guy too. There were times when he didn't say much but, when he did, his remarks would be cutting, funny and straight to the point. When he was interviewed on the television he spoke well, straight and, to paraphrase Oscar Wilde, he could talk without actually saying anything. There was never any off the pitch scandals with Alan, unlike many of the game's superstars. That's why he was called Mary Poppins by our chairman. I know many see that as an insult, but it was a compliment, when you think about it, because he was without any skeletons in his cupboard. He was a great role model for kids and professionals alike.

Shearer and Ginola clashed on the odd occasion. Why? Maybe David's work ethic wasn't as strong as Alan's. They were both superstars; they were both strong willed; strong personalities and their own men. They were both different in their own way. I remember once in the changing room after a game where David got quite animated. He jumped up and waved his finger at Alan and screamed, 'Fuck you Shearer, who do you think you are? You fucking bastard!' I didn't hear what Alan had said but David was furious. Alan didn't react at all, he just laughed and said 'good one!' This wound up Ginola even more because he didn't bite and it didn't seem to bother him. We were all astounded when it happened because someone had sworn at Shearer. We all had great respect for him so no one spoke to him like that.

When we got back home, from our tour of the Far East, the gaffer asked would I mind taking part in a photo session for the newspapers and match day programme. I wasn't aware of what was planned or who was involved but I was happy to oblige. I turned up and it was Alan. The photographers wanted some pictures of our new striker shooting. Man, he hit the ball so ferociously that one shot brought blood to the surface on my arm! He's shouting, 'Howay man, Pav, my daughter could stop these.' I'm telling you, it hurt like hell. And he's shouting, 'Come on, Pav, can you stop this, and this, and this!' When we finished, the gaffer, who was watching the proceedings like a proud father from the sidelines, said, 'Well done lads, go and get a shower.' I went into the dressing room and I couldn't take my shirt off at first. When I did eventually peel it off, I looked in the mirror and I was red, black and blue all over. I even had the sponsor imprint off the ball tattooed on me! I thought, I'm not going in the showers looking like this, Alan will take the piss! So I did a few stretches for 15 minutes and waited until he finished before I had a shower.

Alan was extremely influential in the dressing room. He was very vociferous and encouraging towards all the lads before we went out. When he said something, you listened. He had a lot of respect in the changing room. You didn't want to let him down and you wanted to do well for him. It would have more effect if Alan was shouting and encouraging than someone else. Venners was especially good at doing this as well.

Faustino Asprilla was another great character. I'm not sure what he made of Shearer's arrival at the club. But he was always asking Alan where and what time he had to be at training after every session. Shearer would tell him everything but the truth. Consequently our Colombian striker was always late and got fined.

Tino was always pretending to be ignorant of everything, yet I knew he was aware of all that was going on. There were times when I'd ask him for something and he would reply, 'I don't understand you and don't know what you want.' There were other times when I would be talking to one of the lads and he'd interrupt. He'd say, 'Pav?' I would say, 'What?' Then he would say, 'Fuck you!' in his funny cartoon voice. I'd just shake my head. He was hilarious. He had a real dry sense of humour. There was another time when the gaffer was a bit late so Tino stepped in and did an outstanding impression of him naming the team before the kick off. But Kevin walked in behind Tino while he was in full flow and stood and watched it all. We were crying with laughter. Tino thought we were laughing at his take on Keegan but he was unaware he was standing behind him. When he realised something was up and turned to see Kevin, he humbly apologised.

I never saw Tino get angry or upset with anyone. But he had a fantastic sense of humour. He never said much but when he did he would have you in hysterics. Everybody loved Tino, although I think the residents of Darras Hall were happy to see the back of him and his partying. On the pitch he would be a genius for about an hour, performing tricks, nutmegs and running rings around defenders and then, all of a sudden, he would switch off and lose interest. That was Tino all over.

Some people might say that Kevin may not have done his homework on Asprilla because, like Ginola, he never tracked back. But you can always carry one or two flair players if you have a few grafters in the team. When Dalglish first came in Tino got more games because he found a formula to give him a free role with Ferdinand and Shearer. But the downside to that was Beardsley and Ginola were dropped.

Shearer may have been our only signing that season but he wasn't the only new arrival at St James' Park. After what seemed like years of hammering our defensive fragilities, Mark Lawrenson was offered a defensive coach's position by the gaffer. I remember Alan Hansen saying on Match of the Day, what a fantastic new appointment Mark Lawrenson was for Newcastle. A month later, I'm thinking, yeah, good one Hansen. Since your mate came in we've never won a game or kept a clean sheet. He did a few things with the defence, none that I can remember.

I know I have said we go into every new season with renewed optimism but that wasn't the case until we signed Alan Shearer. It certainly gave us a boost ahead of the Charity Shield. Usually the Premier League champions take on the FA Cup winners. But since Man U won both competitions last term we were invited to provide the double winners the opposition on the Premier League's traditional curtain raiser. The whole occasion was an anti-climax and we really let down our fans, who were magnificent, once again, despite a 4-0 defeat. I'm thinking here we go again and where do we go from here? It was my first and only appearance at Wembley. I don't have any fond memories England's famous showcase arena because not only did we lose the Charity Shield, in the home of English football, but I saw the Czech Republic lose to Germany in the Euro final less than two months previously.

I was on the bench for the club's opening fixture of the new campaign, a match we lost 2-0 at Everton. But I was back in goal for the following game at St James' Park against Wimbledon which we won 2-0. Shearer scored a 20 yard swerving free-kick to net his first goal for the club, although our £15m new signing had a perfectly good goal ruled out at Goodison Park the week before. It was a tremendous goal and a fitting statement of intent from our world class striker.

I remember the first derby game at Sunderland in 1996 when none of our supporters were allowed in to watch the Premier League new boys. I had a few friends and family inside the ground because players still got complimentary tickets for every match. My friend and his wife from the Czech Republic were at the game. I never really gave it much thought but I'd kitted them out in some Newcastle United coats the week before and they decided to walk up to the game in our club colours. I saw him in the stands when I was warming up and nearly shit myself. I'm screaming at him, 'Take the jacket off! Take it off!' He just waved back. It was like a comedy sketch. I repeated, bellowing at the top of my voice, in Czech, 'Take the jacket off! Take the jacket off!' I thought, someone is going to kill him. He's not going to get out of the stadium alive. He eventually cottoned on and took it off. He later told me he got all sorts of abuse from the Sunderland fans but they never beat him up. He probably got away with it because he couldn't speak English.

It might sound a strange thing to say but it was a great game and one of the last matches to be played at Roker Park. The atmosphere was quite intimidating. You could almost feel the hate and venom spilling over onto the pitch from the terraces. Shearer was getting all sorts of abuse. The Sunderland supporters were telling our £15m striker that he wasn't very good, or words to that effect. Come on lads, I think you may have got that call wrong. We hadn't won many games on enemy soil at the time, although our recent form was good against them, so it was great to beat the Mackems.

Martin Scott netted from the penalty spot to give the hosts a 1-0 lead before two headers from Peter Beardsley and Les Ferdinand wrapped up the points. I remember the game well. As the clock was running down I started dribbling in the last minute of the match. We were 2-1 up, and our players and Keegan were screaming at me to clear it. I took the player on before clearing a long ball up field. People might think I'm crazy but I got a thrill out of. Life doesn't get much better than this. Winning 2-1 on the ground of your bitterest rivals and showing the paying public I had a bit of skill was the cherry on the cake. I wasn't showboating or taking the piss. I never took the piss when I was dribbling with the ball. I was always comfortable with the ball at my feet and enjoyed the challenge of taking on a player. I preferred doing that to kicking it out for a corner or a throw in. Surely it's better to clear the ball down the other end of the pitch away from danger than give a team another chance in the last third. The supporters loved it as well and it gave me a big buzz when they cheered me on. But I did this all of my career even when I played for the national team. My brother would be saying, 'Oh no he's going to get caught out and give me a heart attack,' but I never did.

The following day in training Keegan pulled me to one side and said, 'Pav, everybody has seen you do this now. It was the talking point on Sky and in the papers about your dribbling. Be careful in future because everyone will be looking out for you now.' I remember Alan Hansen talking about it on *Match of the Day*, saying how brave I was. It's probably the only positive thing he has ever said about me.

We put quite a run together after the stuttering start of two defeats in our opening three league games; three defeats if you count the Charity Shield. We won seven league games in a row including the 5-0 triumph over Man United at St James' Park. Was it the greatest game or the best result I was ever involved in as a Newcastle player? Possibly, when you consider the quality of the opposition we faced that day. But there were other games such as Antwerp away when Rob Lee scored a hat-trick of headers in a 5-0 victory. We had never beaten Sir Alex Ferguson's side in my time at the club. But on that day we played them off the park. Darren Peacock, Ginola, big Les and Alan scored, Philippe Albert's outrageous chip, provided the coup de gras. Yet the game could've been so different had the referee not been on top of his game. My international colleague Karel Porbosky dived over me to try and win a penalty but Steve Dunn waved it away.

Man U had a bad spell after this, losing three in a row while Peter Schmeichel played poorly, so I'm led to believe. Yes it was a famous victory but they still went on to win the title. I'd rather we won 1-0 and claimed the league championship than win 5-0. We won the battle but not the war. And the following week we went to Leicester, played poorly and lost 2-0. That is why we didn't win the title. We couldn't raise our game for lower league teams. We failed to capitalise on a few games to struggling sides that term.

The team had a good run in the UEFA Cup this season. We despatched Halmstads of Sweden in the first round, before overcoming Ferencvaros in the second round. The 4-0 score line in our home leg suggests we romped to victory in a game, where Ginola netted an absolute cracker. But the Hungarians provided tough opposition, certainly in the first leg where they beat us 3-2.

In the third round we faced French opposition. I remember I dropped a cross in the away leg at Metz, which Keegan wasn't happy about, after Peter Beardsley put us 1-0 up from the penalty spot. I think David Ginola got fouled. Two late Tino goals ensured we got through to the quarter finals against Monaco. Both were typical Asprilla strikes. One was an instinctive header after Darren Peacock put the ball back across the box. The Columbia international celebrated by hanging his shirt on the corner flag at the Gallowgate End. The second was sublime. He drew the defender, fainted one way, then went the other before delightfully chipping the oncoming goalkeeper. It was exhibition football.

Unfortunately, Tino's corner flag shenanigans proved costly. He got booked for it and consequently ruled out of our quarter final clash against Monaco at St James' Park. Both Shearer and Ferdinand were missing through injury and we were a bit toothless up front. We eventually lost 1-0 before crashing 3-0 in the south of France. Once again, it was a tournament we felt we could win. We never seemed to get the rub of the green or that little bit luck that would've seen us land a trophy. Although I thought it was a bit strange, former manager Ruud Gullit having a priest bless St James' Park because he thought it was cursed, I still understood it.

When Keegan quit, Newcastle tried to bring in Sir Bobby Robson, who was manager at Barcelona. But he wanted to honour his contract at the Camp Nou. It was just my luck. Had he took the job then, maybe my career would've turned out much better. Unfortunately, it got even worse for me. Pedro let me know he feared the worse when Dalglish was linked with the job. The little magician made it known he never got on with Kenny and knew his days were numbered at the club. He said he was a dead man walking. Kenny tried to destroy his career at Liverpool. There were a few people at the club, at the time, who voiced similar sentiments.

First impressions last and I wasn't very impressed by the Scot when he was introduced to us at the training ground. The session was interrupted as the chairman came onto the pitch and presented the Scotsman to us. He went around shaking the hands of the players. When he walked towards me, he shook my hand and wished me 'good luck'. He didn't even look me in the eye. I thought why is he wishing me good luck? It sounded sarcastic, the way he said it. This was a man who had won dozens of trophies as a player and manager and commanded respect throughout the world. I was expecting something more like, 'Hello, I'm Kenny, the new manager. I'm looking forward to working with you.' But no, nothing like that.

Training was really disappointing under Kenny. He never seemed to be taking any notice of what was happening, who was training hard or who wasn't putting a shift in. He would be laughing and joking with Terry Mac on the sidelines. This was day in and day out. I hated it. I have always been a good professional and didn't like it when someone wasn't taking it seriously, and those two weren't taking it seriously. I felt it was disrespectful. There's a time and place for a laugh and a joke and I didn't feel this was the right time. There were no tactics and they never got involved until we started playing the matches at the end.

Supporters were still coming into to watch us train when he first became manager but he stopped them not long after he took over. By the start of his first full season in charge, no fans were allowed in at all.

Pedro, Ginola and I were always in the big noses' team. That is what everyone called us. I don't know who gave us the nickname but it stuck. We always won, yet none of us could get a game on a Saturday. No one could beat us in Kenny's time. It wasn't just me who had this feeling but Pedro and Ginola, two of the best players to ever don the black and white shirt. I didn't mind Dalglish not liking or rating me as a goalkeeper. It was the lack of respect. And I wasn't the only one. He was the same with Darren Peacock, Philippe Albert, John Beresford and Rob Lee. I couldn't believe it at half time in one game when he tore into Rob. We thought he liked him. Yet there he was, tearing into one of Newcastle's best players. Dalglish quickly lost respect in the dressing room with typical behaviour like this.

It was not a surprise when Pedro and David moved on at the end of the season. Beardsley went to Bolton and Ginola went to Tottenham. I know I put in a transfer request when I was at the club, but I never ever wanted to leave. I was happy with everything about life at Newcastle, other than the times when I wasn't in the team.

I was back in the first XI for the last four matches of the season. I can't remember the reason why Dalglish put me back in. Maybe he wanted to see me in first team action or wasn't too keen on Shaka, I don't know. I do know I kept four clean sheets and we had conceded goals in the previous five fixtures before I got back in. It helped us qualify for the Champions League. We qualified because we had a better goal difference than Liverpool and Arsenal. We all had the same points.

The 5-0 home victory over Forest on the last day of the season and results not going well for our rivals was a fitting end to a turbulent campaign. The fact that our North-East rivals, Middlesbrough and Sunderland, got relegated was the cherry on the cake for our supporters. What a change from finishing runners up last term. Last season it was as if we had been relegated yet this time it felt like we had won the league, such was the contrast of emotions.

I was back as the club's number one and I thought I deserved it. The praise the team and I were getting was great. And obviously we got a good bonus for it. It was like Groundhog Day or déjà vu because I had been here several times in the past. The sad aspect of finishing runners up and helping Newcastle into the Champions League for the first time in their history, I never got a game in it. I only got as far as the bench.

It was another eventful season at St James' Park and a one to reflect on what might have been. I felt we were unlucky once again not pick up some silverware. And I seriously believe had we not been without Alan Shearer for a large part of the season we could have won, not only the UEFA Cup but Premier League title. It was also a season where we saw a changing of the guard with Kenny Dalglish replacing Kevin Keegan in a similar way to what he did as a player at Liverpool in the 1970s. Unfortunately, things were never the same with Dalglish in charge. The club has gone backwards and never recovered from when he was appointed.

CHAPTER 10
PAVEL IS A BAIRN

It goes without saying, we were poor. Life growing up in Bohumin was everything you could imagine a forgotten village or an unremarkable backwater to be in a Communist state: tough, brutal and hard. Imagine Ken Loach meeting Mike Leigh to discuss making my autobiography into a Dickensian black comedy set in the Czech Republic. I'm joking of course. I mean, people would think it was a work of fiction rather than a factual portrayal of my life. I don't want to paint too bleak a picture of growing up in the Czech Republic, with thousands walking the streets in threadbare clothes and starving of hunger, because my childhood was very happy. No one had any money, everyone was the same and we didn't know any different. We thought everyone outside Czechoslovakia was in a similar position, although it would be fair to say we didn't really think about anyone outside our village, town or country. But I still look back fondly on my childhood; even the times when I had to wear girls' clothing.

I still get embarrassed when I think back to when my mother made me wear my sisters' clothes. It wasn't quite *The Rocky Horror Picture Show*, but all the same. People will laugh when they read this but, I was a boy and, I didn't want to wear girls' clothing. It wasn't very funny back then. I felt a bit girly. It was uncomfortable. Some days I had to wear a red coat with a dark blue or pink stripe. Don't get me wrong, it was a nice jacket, for a girl! I didn't wear a skirt though. I would have refused to do that. I'd say, 'Mam, I'm not wearing those clothes.' And she would reply, 'But Pavel, you have to because I don't have anything else for you to wear and it is cold outside.' I can understand, looking back, because there were five children and we were probably the poorest in the village where we lived. Other families were better off because, they either didn't have as many children or, the parents had better paid jobs.

I was born, in Bohumin, which is about five miles from Ostrava. Bohumín, a town, for those with an interest in the past, lies in the historical region of Cieszyn Silesia, near to the border of Poland. It is split into two: Old Bohumin and industrial New Bohumin, while several villages are administratively part of the town. The majority of people living there now are Czech, but there are a small number of Polish residents because of the town's historical past. Many inhabitants have links to the country through their ancestors. Before World War II, the town was inhabited by a large German community, but now the city is widely known as having the largest community of Romani people in the Czech Republic.

It developed from little more than a village, in the Middle Ages, to evolve into an industrial town; eventually becoming under control of the Austrian Empire and Austria-Hungary in the 19th century. After that it became somewhat of a political football. Poland and Germany both gained possession, before and between the wars, before it was restored to Czechoslovakia in 1945.

My mother, Bernadette Lambert Srnicek, still lives in the house, in Bohumin, where I was brought up and that is where my family, my brother and sisters, all go to visit her. My brother, Milan, was born in 1973, and my sisters: Maria, 1960, Bozena, 1961 and Eliska, 1970. My mother was brought into the world in 1942, in France, but came to Czechoslovakia when she was three years old because her mother married a Czech. She didn't know much French or Czech, for that matter, because her parents never sent her to school. Conceived into a large family of nine children, my mother has worked hard all her life from an early age

My father was called Pavol (the Slovak spelling). He was born in 1932 and, ironically, died on my birthday in 2004, which has now turned into a sad day for me. I can't celebrate it. There are a few coincidences surrounding his death, which have made me uncomfortable. For example, he was 72, while I was 36, so I was half his age. The year 2004 was also the same year my son, Maxim, was born. My father never got to see my youngest child, who was two months old at the time, because we were living in Italy. There is an old saying that with death there is life and vice versa and I think there could be something in that. But I feel as if my father was trying to say something to me before he died; trying to send a message. I'm sure of it. I don't know what the message is yet, but I'll work it out. Another link is that my sister was born on March 11 and he died on March 10. There just seem too many coincidences related to me and maybe my son.

I was brought up a Catholic but I am not a religious fanatic, although I am quite a spiritual person. I went to church as child with my grandmother and sometimes saw the priest after school, so I respected the institution. I believe there is something there after we die, although I don't know what. I would not argue with other people who have a different faith to mine. I respect their religious belief and would like to think one day all other religions will find a similar tolerance in the future. I think everyone should have some faith.

My parents met in Hostalkovy, which is close to a city called Krnov. They came across each other on a farm which was owned by the Government. At the time Czechoslovakia was a Communist country so the Government owned or ran everything. My parents worked on a farm all of their lives, and while my mother was feeding the pigs and looking after the animals, such as the cows, my father was employed as a wood cutter or drove a tractor. Eventually they left and moved to Bohumin, because my father had a few problems with people in that part of the country. He was a bit aggressive, when he was a young man, and it was common practice for him to get into fights with some of the locals.

There were the odd benefits from my parents working on a farm, such as cheaper milk. I used to get up at 3am on some days to help my mother on the farm because it was heavy work. On the other hand, if her shift was in the afternoon, I would go and help her after football training. She had about 60 cows to milk a day. And not only that, she had to clean them, sort out the big bales of hay and clean their sleeping quarters. My mother was an incredibly strong woman and it is just as well because she had to do the work. Still, I wanted to help and ease her workload. Then I would go back home, have a shower and go to school. And because of the type of work involved that comes with labouring on a farm, I used to stink to high heaven. Even after I had a shower you could smell the pigs, cows and farm on me. The kids at school could smell me too and they would say, 'You fucking stink! Have you been working with your mam?' I did that between the ages of 13 to 16 years old. It is no wonder I used to stink most of the time.

The food we ate was pretty bland and basic. We always had bread, milk and cheese, as we didn't have much money. We knew on the days when we had just milk and potatoes for lunch or dinner, money was in short supply. On days when there was a bit of cash around we would have chicken. My mother always bought my father the best food because he was the family breadwinner. It was always in the fridge and we couldn't touch it. But, saying that, he didn't like to see us go without good food so when he was eating chicken or salami etc he would share it with us.

It's ironic I became a professional sportsman, or rather a footballer, because there were no sportsmen in our family. I am the only one. My father hated sports, while my mother never had a chance to play them. So I was never inspired by anyone other than myself. Sport helped me to escape from the hardships that life brought in a Communist country.

I started to play football when I was seven, although the state officially banned children from playing competitive sports until they were nine. I wasn't to know this at the time, but I believe this was the first in a long line of barriers or obstructions to stop me playing sport or progressing in my career. Nevertheless, I was better than most kids my age so I always got asked to play football with the older children. You needed a registration document to officially play but I always played on someone else's card. And because I was two years younger than the other children I played with, it meant I was the smallest. The unwritten kids' rule at the time was that the smallest person went in nets. But because I was good in goal it did not matter. Secondly, the team were happy for me to stay between the posts because I was much better than the kids who were much older than I.

My father and I clashed several times in my young life about playing sports or football. And, regrettably, because of that, my father never ever saw me play, in the Premier League or for the Czech Republic, which was another sad aspect of my life. The catalyst for this was probably seeing me get kicked in the head when I played in goal as a ten-year-old child. He saw what happened, yet didn't come over to see if I was OK. He just walked away. When I got home he gave me one hell of a beating. It's mad when you think about it. I get injured and then I get a good hiding! He screamed 'I'm not going to watch you play ever again, because someone will kill you! You will not play that sport again!' However, as you know, I continued to play.

Years later when I was about to make my debut for the Czech Republic, I thought maybe he would have mellowed so I asked whether he would come and watch me play. He refused. He never saw a live game, but I have been told, subsequently, my father saw it on the television. And talking of television; I never had the luxury of a coloured television until I joined the army and got married, around 1988. We only had a black and white TV at my parents' home. Other

My father Pavol as I remember him.

Me and my sister Eliska after first Holy Communion in church in Bohumin.

Me and my neighbor Petr with my first football, I was six years old and it was obvious what I was going to be.

Muzi 1975.

Muzi 1976.

Muzi 1979.

This is me at two years of age. Already the makings of a great haircut.

This is the main entrance of my village stadium.

Life in the army with Dukla Prague. Here I am in army uniform with my friend Rosta Prokop, who was centre half for both Dukla and Banik Ostrava.

My army team Dukla Tabor.

In goal for Dukla Tabor.

Reserve team Banik Ostrava.

This is me with famous goalkeeper and goalkeeping coach Ivo Viktor and first choice keeper Petr Kostelnik at my army club Dukla Praha where I moved to from Dukla Tabor.

This was my first goalkeeper coach Lojza Pavelka who still lives in my village.

This is the photo where I'm wearing my sisters blue jacket with pink stripes. I'm the one on the far right, at the back. Thankfully the photo is in black and white.

A wonderful moment for me. My return to St James' Park. I came on as a substitute for Shay Given with two minutes remaining.

The highs and lows at Newcastle United and the colourful array of shirts I was asked to wear. Best days of my life.

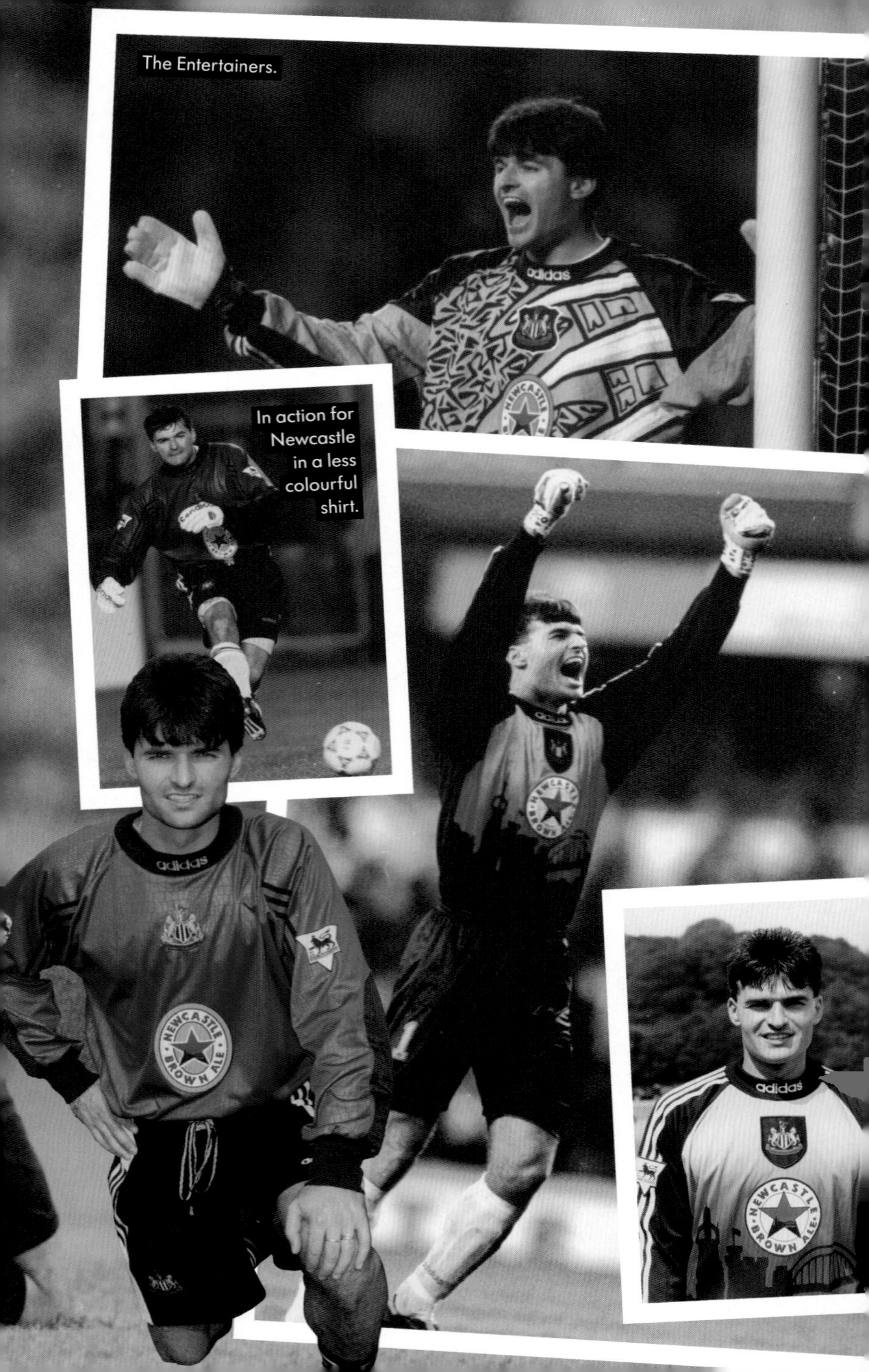

The Entertainers.

In action for Newcastle in a less colourful shirt.

In goal for Dukla Tabor.

My spell at Sheffield Wednesday.

Maxim and Vendy.

Vendy.

Ready before a game with Vendy and my mam when she visited England for the first time.

Me and my closest friend Petr Cavos in Army Dukla Praha.

Reserve team of Dukla Praha, (the child on the photo is not mine).

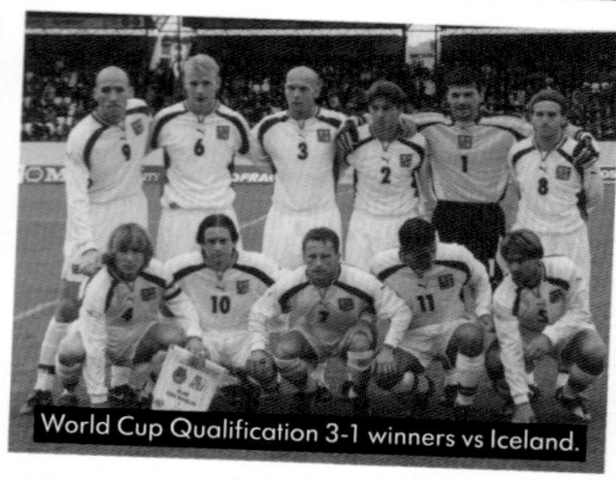
World Cup Qualification 3-1 winners vs Iceland.

Pavel Srnicek Goalkeepers Academy, this time for Czech boys. We relax playing golf in Czech Republic.

Pavel Srnicek Goalkeepers Academy, this w
my first year as a coach. It was for a group
English boys in Czech Repub

families had them. Again, it was because we were poor.

My father was diagnosed with prostate cancer, 20 years before he died, so he had to manage it. And because of this he never wanted to travel very far. He was more comfortable stopping at home. He used to like a drink and the doctors allowed him to have a little. But I think the cancer turned him into an alcoholic. Maybe the reason I don't drink is because of my father. It turned him into a monster at times. He used to beat my brother, sisters and I, when he was drunk.

I can't say I had a poor relationship with my father. He would have laid down his life for our family. He was originally from Slovakia and we used to go and visit his family in the holiday seasons. If my brother, sisters or I asked for anything and he had the money, he would buy whatever we wanted. He was generous from that perspective. Then there were other times when he used to drink a lot and we got nothing. It's true he wasn't a loving person, in a tactile sense, the way I am with my children. I want to hug and kiss my children but I don't think my father's generation did that. That didn't make him a bad man.

My father hated seeing my sisters or any of us walking around the house in our underwear. But as kids we never thought there was anything wrong in parading around in our undies. We always had to be dressed in our clothes. I think this was because he was from a big family and that was how he was brought up. We lived in a big flat but it was quite cramped, I suppose, because we also had my grandmother living with us. It wasn't quite like the Brady Bunch, The

Waltons or Snow White and the Seven Dwarves, but my mother and father slept in a big bed alone while all of us children slept together in the same bed.

It may sound as if I had a bad life as child but I didn't. I still had fun because I had sport. There was a sports club next to my house. There were tennis courts; football pitches and a lake. In the morning I would be off first thing to play and then back in the evening. My brother, Milan, played a bit of sport: head tennis and badminton very well but he, like the rest of my family, weren't that interested in playing at a higher level other than amateur. Then if you had to travel it was tough because no one had any transport.

In the village I was brought up in there was nothing else to do but play sport. I was lucky all my friends felt the same way. There were some talented kids but, unfortunately, I was the only one who made it through to play professional football. There was one player, who played outfield, Tomas Wybraniec, who had the talent but he didn't seem to have the hunger and dedication. And that is probably why he didn't take the next step.

I first started playing for my village football team but later on I played for the school team. I had a dilemma at an early age because there was a sports school in Bohumin. So children with a special talent went there. I was asked to go but I didn't want to go to that school, at first, because I felt it was full of prima donnas. I was the only player from the local school who played for the village team. The rest of the team was made up from kids who went to the sports school.

It seemed I was up against it even at that early age. When the area sports day came around, the sports school always won most of the athletics competitions, although we still won the odd contest. I played for the basketball, volleyball, head tennis and decathlon teams, and my school always used to win those contests. I was also skilled at weightlifting and could've taken that up as a sport. I think children today miss this variety of sport. Even now, and I am in my late 40s, when I take my goalkeepers down the beach for volleyball, the coaches and I always beat the youngsters who are half our age. And, because of that, the chairman of that school came back and asked me to join. He told me there would be greater advantages for me if I was to change schools.

We had one bicycle in the family and when my father came home from work I would take it to go to training. It's probably how I got so fit. I started training at 3pm and he came in at 2.40, so I only had 20 minutes to get to the train station, which was four miles away. It caused much merriment with the lads, when they seen me peddling like a madman. They used to joke 'you have already had one session'. It was hard but fun and I look back nostalgically on the time. But then I was always stressed to whether I would make it at all and whether my father would be back from work on time.

My parents never took any interest in my education. My father, for example, never once looked at my school books or work. He only ever signed my homework once. My mother always used to do it apart from that one time. They were never interested on how I was doing at school because they never went themselves.

My father couldn't write at the time and today, my mother cannot read or write. My parents said, 'We don't know anything about school. You'll have to help yourself.' For example, we used to have a marking system where you would get graded one to five: one being the best grade and five being the worst. I once came in with a five and she asked if I could do any better? Other children came in to school the following day with stories of how they had been beaten by their parents for such poor marks or grades. It didn't mean anything to my mother or father. They couldn't give a monkeys' about my schooling. Later on my sisters helped me with my homework when I was struggling.

I was reasonably academic. I wasn't the smartest kid in the school but I could do the work without any real problems. One year I had five 'two' grades in my subjects, which were the best results in my year. I didn't really have any problems at school until I was older and I missed days and days of schooling because I got excused to play football. I neglected my studies, however, and when I got to high school, to concentrate more on football. The teachers often complained that my grades weren't good enough or getting any better. But I told them they had to cut me some slack because I was representing the school in several sports and couldn't give 100 per cent to both studies and sport, it was impossible.

When I left school, I went to train in the fabric industry and play for their football team, TJ ZD Bohumin, in the second division of the Czech Republic League. So I started work at 6am and stayed there until 9am before I went to training. We couldn't turn professional because it was a Communist country, remember. So in your book, or your papers, you were identified by your job, such as a miner, painter or fabric worker. And you played football for the industry you were employed in. I worked on a metal lathe, a bit like an engineer I suppose. I did that from the ages of 15 to 18 and then went into the army.

CHAPTER 11
STOP OR I'LL SHOOT!

Banik Ostrava were the team I supported as a boy, simply because they were the closest team to my village. I wasn't really aware of any other football club outside of the Czech Republic, because television exposure to anything beyond our country was limited. We only got to see what the Government wanted us to watch. I had no idea about Newcastle United, Manchester United or the giants of Italy, Germany or France.

I got more of an idea about life outside our village, town and home nation when I was 17 and received a call to play in the Czech Republic under-21s. This is a story in itself. The manager of the under-21s, Karel Bruckner, was also the boss of a top tier Czech team at the time, Sigma Olomouc. Bruckner went on to manage the national side and also took charge of the Austria team for two years. Anyway, Bruckner wanted to sign me for Sigma, but the Banik chairman refused to let me go. And as a consequence of that he told my chairman he wouldn't be selecting me for the under-21s anymore. I played only three times, the last of which was a 4-0 win over Iceland. This was another example of someone putting a hurdle in my way. And it wasn't of my own doing. It was nothing to do with my ability or personality, more a political act by one person to spite another.

When I was 17-years-old, Banik approached me and asked whether I would like to join the team I supported, but I was unsure for several reasons. The club's under-19 coach had seen me play for TJ ZD Bohumin and liked what he saw. He then came to my house to see my parents. My folks didn't really have a clue what was going on. But the agent explained the situation clear enough to them; was complimentary about my ability and asked my parents for permission to sign me. My father, being my father, was blunt with the agent and made it known he had no idea what I got up too outside of the house. My mother was a bit more encouraged by what the agent had to say and gave her blessing. But, at the end of the day, it was my decision to make and I refused them three times before I eventually relented and signed.

Why did I refuse to sign for them? In essence, I was ashamed to go to Ostrava because of my poor background. I was the local boy from the village and had never been in a big town like Ostrava. Remember I was the boy who wore his sister's clothes. All the other boys had Adidas trainers. I didn't have any so called designer shoes, trainers or boots, for that matter. I didn't get my first pair of jeans until I was 15. And I had to slave for a month with some local workmen to build a crematorium before I saved enough money to buy the jeans. Ironically, my father was eventually laid to rest in the very same building I helped to construct. He was laid in the chapel of rest, with the coffin open. I remember saying my final goodbye before he was taken away to be buried. I spent a little time explaining that I had helped construct the building. These were the last words I spoke to him and it was an emotional time for me.

In the end the manager of the village team talked me around and persuaded me to leave. He explained that I was a big a fish in a small pond and, if I was going to make a bigger splash, I had to join Ostrava to realise my ambitions and dreams. My father didn't have a clue about how good I was until his friends told him in the pub. I think it was the first time he'd really taken an interest in my football. He returned from the ale house more positive than he'd ever been before. He said if I was as good as people were saying then why didn't I go? On the other hand, my mother was worried about me leaving home, despite it only being about three miles away. I think my mother thought three miles was Newcastle to London, rather than Gosforth to Newcastle. Then there was the expense. We didn't have any money and it cost around 3,000 Korunas, which was about £50 back then, to go on a pre-season tour. I told the coach my parents did not have that sort of money because there were five children at home. They took all of this into consideration and in the end the club paid for me because they felt I was a valuable enough commodity to invest in.

I went straight into the first team. I didn't have to do apprentice chores, like they had in England at the time. We had kit men who washed the strips and training gear. We used to clean our own boots, but that was it. I used to get two sets of gloves a season and I had to look after them. If I didn't, it was tough. There was no money to buy new gloves.

Like I mentioned earlier, most teams were sponsored by an industry and Banik Ostrava was no different. They were sponsored by the local mining company. So my job card didn't say professional footballer, it was miner. We all went down the mines for some work experience to see how they did their job. But that's all we did. We weren't down the mines doing hard labour like the rest of the manual workers. One of the most difficult parts of my job, or most embarrassing, was picking up my wages. I had to queue up in line every month at the same time as the working miners to pick up my money. They all knew the footballers did fuck all, but kick a stupid ball around, and get paid for it. I felt sorry for the people who had to graft relentlessly down there while I was getting good money as a teenager. My first wage was 5,000 Korunas, which was about £100 a month. To measure how silly this was, my parents only made 8,000 Korunas a month between them. I tried to help my family with a bit of money but later on it got more difficult because I had to look after my own family.

The wage structure at the time was 3,000 for new players, 5,000 for players who had established themselves in the first team and, finally, 7,000, which was for players who played for the national team. The manager caused a bit of a stir because he announced to the team that I would be in the middle tier wage band, despite being a new player. The experienced professionals were saying, 'Gaffa, he's done fuck all! We've had to play for five years to get that money and he hasn't played five minutes!' The manager thought he could justify it because he believed I was good enough to play at that level. There were several players who didn't like me, but I didn't care. I was happy. I got a new flat from the club, free from rent, although I had to pay for the electricity. But that was everyone who worked for the company.

I was with Banik for less than a year before I got conscripted into the army. It was fun while it lasted but

I couldn't avoid doing my time in the army. Every young boy had to do two years national service and I was no different. There was no transfer fee; I was just expected to join up. I know this might be a bit confusing, but like I explained earlier, for example, that Banik was a mining team, there were other football clubs run by the fabric industry or cotton business, or engineering etc, the army had football clubs as well. In my case, the army club I joined was Dukla Tabor. Dukla were a second tier outfit in the Czech Republic League who attracted about 500 supporters for every home game.

I was due to join up in June of 1987, but Dukla asked if I could come two months ahead of schedule, in April. I thought I could work this in my favour so I negotiated an agreement to go early if I could get married first. So I got married on April 4 and joined the army on April 6. I even arranged a deal to borrow some extra money from the club to get married because I didn't have any cash. I needed the money for wedding party and the rings etc.

The Czech people were never fearful of another war. They knew, because the country was so small, they wouldn't really have any major involvement. National service was just part of our life and culture following the war until just after the Velvet Revolution. Eventually it went from two years to one and then you didn't have to enrol. After that if you wanted to be in the army you would join up and it would be your job.

The Velvet Revolution took place in 1989. It was a non violent protest against 41 years of a one party Communist government. Subsequently, the protest saw

Czechoslovakia become a parliamentary republic. The country went through several changes throughout its short history, until its peaceful dissolution into the Czech Republic and Slovakia in 1993. One of the more dramatic changes saw the nation incorporated into Nazi Germany during World War II. The country was democratically run between the wars before becoming under Communist rule, until Democracy was restored in 1989.

I got promoted to Dukla Prague, a year later, because I was Tabor's player of the year and the general at Dukla asked for me. Once again, there was no transfer fee. I just packed my kit and off I went. Dukla had crowds of about 2,000. In fact Dukla are quite well know in Britain thanks to indie band Half Man Half Biscuit, who had a minor hit with All I Want for Christmas is a Dukla Prague Away Kit. It was on their album Back Again in DHSS. Dukla were one of the best clubs in Czech Republic League.

I had to get up at 4am or 6am to do my chores; sometimes it is something as laborious as peeling potatoes for 1000 men. Then shower, back for breakfast and do a training session. Then back in for lunch and another session after that. Then I would be out at 9pm for more army chores like checking people were in their barracks, houses or on guard. If you found people wandering about you would ask them what their number is. The day you join the army everyone gets given the number 730. The number represents every day you have to spend in the army i.e. 730 days or two years. For every day you spend in the army you reduce that number. For example, after a day it will be 729, then 728 and so on until you're down to no number. You always suffered if you went to the kitchen at meal times and the chef would ask you your number. The higher the number, the less food you got because you were held in low esteem. This used to piss us off so we eventually turned this around in our favour. The kitchen staff liked to play football and didn't have a ball, so when they came into our hut asking to borrow our ball, we would say 'OK, as long as you start giving us more food.' It worked. I did a lot of this when I was at Dukla Tabor, but not Dukla Prague.

The first 30 days in the army is tough. It is all military school with guns and war games. You have to pass this stage. It is very rigorous, severe and strict. Cleaning guns; stripping them down; putting them back together; setting out your clothes; getting changed within 30 seconds and cleaning your boots. Punishments were generally cleaning the house, press ups etc. But they didn't punish the individual, it was the whole group. I couldn't run away from this army camp, like at Dukla Prague later on, because we were fenced in with armed guards and dogs protecting the compound. At Dukla Prague we had our own house with three floors, where all the sportsmen stayed: footballers, athletes and handball players. It was like a hotel with one security guard on the door so we could just walk into town or training no problem. We couldn't get changed into our civvies' clothes. We always had to wear an army tracksuit in the house; on the training ground and outside, only our army uniform. There was no one checking on us. If I could've run away, from the army in Dukla Tabor, I would have.

I got caught once at Dukla Prague and was thrown in a prison cell for three days. It was brutal. Man... that was the most uncomfortable three days of my life. The floor was made of marble and so cold that you couldn't sit on it. There was no chair. You had to stand all day because the bench you slept on is bolted to the wall during the day. The food was awful, bread; stew with a bit of meat and some water. I think Chinese water torture would've been kinder or an hour listening to The Birdie Song. I was threatened with proper prison if I did it again. My coach, at the time, Koldic, who was the highest ranking officer, was screaming at me. He was furious and I was shitting myself.

My time in prison was suspended for a short while because we had a small tour in Italy planned, to play in a tournament. I got off lightly to be honest. God knows how long I would have done in prison had I not been player of the competition. The coach threatened me with longer. He told me I was a lucky man and said the sentence would've been tougher had I not performed well. He reckoned I helped give Dukla Prague a good name abroad. The consequences of going to jail are sevenfold. If you go, you don't get promoted, you don't get a salary increase and you're life is buggered, basically! I had one stripe on my arm before prison, and I was supposed to get a second stripe soon after, but they withdrew it from me as part of my punishments.

I got rumbled the first time, in Dukla Tabor, when I missed the train from home and I had to get a taxi. I asked the driver how much the journey would cost. He said 15,000 Korunas. I thought, fucking hell, that's nearly a year's wages! When the taxi dropped me off at the army camp I was there before any of the lads. I had to ask the driver to wait for the train to arrive and request the lads to chip in because I did not have the money to pay him. When the lads got off the train they were asking what I was doing here. I tried to joke about it and say I fancied coming back early. But then I told them what had happened and needed some money to pay the cab. They called me worse than shit. I eventually paid them all back because I called my Mrs to send some money from our savings. It meant we had no savings left but I couldn't afford to be late again. I got all sorts of grief from the older lads because, remember, we all get punished, not only the guy who has committed the crime, if you like.

There was another time, when I was with Dukla Prague, that I missed the train from my village. I tried to stop the train but it wouldn't halt because I was wearing normal civvies' clothes. Had I been wearing my army clothes the train would've stopped for me. But I wasn't wearing my army uniform because I didn't want anyone to know I was away. So as a consequence I missed a training session. My team mates tried to cover up by telling our superiors that 'he was just here a minute ago' or 'you've just missed him' but they worked it out pretty quickly.

The third and final time, my goalkeeper coach, Ivo Viktor, caught me. I nearly shit myself. Had he grassed me up, that would have been my football career over before it started, so I have a lot to thank him for. When Ivo caught me, it wasn't because I had gone home. I was too scared to try that again after spending time doing porridge. My Mrs, Pavla, came to see me in Prague and he caught the both of us coming out of the metro station. I was wearing civvies' clothes. Had I been wearing my army uniform everything would've been OK. He didn't say anything until after the training session that afternoon. He called me over and asked where I was that morning. I told him I was in the house watching TV. He then started grilling me further, which had me worried. I'm thinking what the fuck is going on here? He then recounted the time, where, when and what we, Pavla and I, were wearing. I'm thinking, I'm fucked here. But then he said, 'If I report this you will go to prison. You know I think a lot of you as a person and a footballer but if you are lying to me I will never forgive you and never help you again.' I then apologised and asked him to forgive me, which he did. Later on he became my coach at the national team. At the time it was a serious incident, but then later on in life we laughed about it. Had it been someone else it could've been so different. I may never have played football again. I could've been reduced to working like an ordinary man. The thought didn't cross my mind at the time. I just wanted to see my wife because I missed her. I was really fortunate beyond belief.

I wasn't the army bad boy. It may sound like I was James Dean, a Rebel Without a Cause, but I wasn't the only one. Everyone, or most of us, tried it on. We all supported each other through the bad times though. It was a good bonding and team building exercise if you like because we were all in the shit. We would telephone each other and mark each other's cards if someone in authority was on the prowl. It was nothing sinister, mainly because we were missing our wives and families, who we would be put up in nearby hotels.

We were away 30 days at a time, locked in a camp learning about army life. It was perfectly natural we wanted to see our wives and families.

There were incentives because when I played for Dukla Tabor, we were struggling in a relegation battle. So the General said for every game we win we would get two days off. We never lost a game after that. Not only that, I was the player of the season that year. I kept loads of clean sheets. The camaraderie was brilliant. Remember I was still the youngster in the team and all the experienced players would jokingly threaten me, saying, 'hey young bird, no goals for the opposition today, we want two days off'. Young bird is what all the younger players were called.

All the younger players were required to act as personal servants, as in 'young bird', to the senior players, in pretty much the same way as the Fagging system in public schools in England. Obviously, when I became a senior player I had a younger player who would run around doing things for me. It was like an unwritten law in the army but it was a tradition passed down from generation to generation and we were expected to uphold it. I was lucky in a lot of respect because I came half way through a season and wasn't allocated a senior player, although I did do small jobs for several players.

Some of them were bastards and some were OK. The bastards would wake you at 2am and order you to get them a glass of water or raise an alarm. Then you'd jump out of your bed and get into your clothes and they'd start laughing, saying there is no alarm and that you can go back to bed. Some would ask what the weight of a letter is and punish you if you didn't know.

I'd say ten kilos and then they would go, 'No, it's 30 kilos. Give me 30 press ups!' Sometimes they'd ask how much water was in the letter they're holding. I'm thinking, what? Water in a letter! They'd say, one litre or two, and whatever answer you chose you'd have to drink that amount in water! It's funny looking back at it now but at the time it was a nightmare.

I nearly shot one of my officers when I was on guard duty. You patrol the premises making sure everything is OK. No one is allowed in or out. There is a procedure to go through if someone appears when you're on guard. You tell them to, 'Stop, shine the torch in your face or I will shoot you.' If the person does not stop on the second, stop, shine the torch in your face or I will shoot, instruction, you have permission to shoot the person involved. First you shoot in the air and then aim for the legs.

Every now and again a major or a captain would make a surprise visit and check in on you, just in case you have fallen asleep at your post. So this time I screamed the command and he wouldn't shine the torch in his face. I cocked the trigger back, so he could hear it. But still nothing and I am shitting myself. I'm thinking, I don't want to kill anyone but, I have to do my duty, so I let go two shots into the sky and the major, checking on me, is screaming, 'It is me! Stop! Don't shoot!' After that I was counting down the days until I left the army. I thought, I don't need any more of these traumas. We were all presented with a dressmaker's measuring metre, of which we would cut 1cm each day for last 100 days until there was none left. Some of the guys would shade in each centimetre with a different colouring pen. Some would shape hearts or different designs with their centimetre. This is a Czech army tradition or ritual. You knew you were on the last furlong of your time in the army. It was a barometer of how long you had left to serve in the army.

There was no party when we left, we just went home. I was glad to leave but army life had its benefits. It taught us discipline, how to be self sufficient and great camaraderie. For example, when we went home on leave we knew that at some stage we would be starving because food was rationed, so we all brought food from home and hid it in our locker. On an evening we would share it amongst ourselves. I brought the pig fat. We had lots of it because my parents worked on a farm. Others brought bread or even onions. I never liked onions but the best food I ever ate when I was starving was bread, pig fat spread and onions. Oh man, it was a pleasure every night. Like Manna from heaven. Now, there is no national service in the Czech Republic, it is a professional job. National service ended in 2004. But I think they should have kept it for discipline, how to be self sufficient and great camaraderie.

I agreed to sign a three year contract with Banik Ostrava, around about Christmas time, four months before I was due to leave Dukla Prague and the army. But I only played for them for one year because I left to go to Newcastle.

CHAPTER 12
MAGPIE TO OWL

My first game for Sheffield Wednesday? No, you couldn't make this stuff up. Irony of ironies, I was to make my Premier League debut against my beloved Magpies, the club I hold dearest to my heart, at St James' Park! Another paradox to this, of course, was that I'd taken my first tentative steps for Newcastle in 1991 against Wednesday. Maybe it was fated that I was to go and play for the Owls. I've always been a spiritual person and a believer in fate.

There were hundreds of things spinning through my head. I was still raw and, if I'm honest, more than a bit bitter about how I left Tyneside. I knew Kenny Dalglish had been sacked and Ruud Gullit was the new boss in his place, but then I see Dalglish's son, Paul, is in the starting line up. I considered smashing into him and taking him out if I got the chance. But then I thought, this is ridiculous, it's not his fault. I was thinking irrationally. I can't blame him because I think his father is a bastard. But this is what was going through my head. The wounds were still open, gaping and very sore. And when I heard the name Dalglish, it was a bit like Pavlov's dogs! I hear the name and it stirred me into such a frenzy that I wanted to kill!

It goes without saying the preparation and lead up to the game was bizarre. I was in the opposition dressing room, wearing the colours of another side and the objective of the afternoon was to beat Newcastle. It just didn't make sense at first. The reception I received from the home faithful was, obviously, nothing short of tremendous. It was the same the following season when we got hammered 8-0 in Sir Bobby Robson's first home game in charge of Newcastle. I was on the bench that day, but when I stood up the fans gave me a fantastic ovation. I had to sit down because I didn't want to embarrass the team or Kevin Pressman.

I had to be professional. There was no other option but to focus on winning for Wednesday. I wanted to play well; prove people wrong and show the club it was a mistake to let me go. After a maelstrom of an afternoon the contest ended all square. I think 1-1 was a fair result. Ironically, Paul Dalglish scored his first and only goal for United after only four minutes. My old team mate Warren Barton hit a bobbling shot from distance and it deflected into the youngster's path and he slotted home from close range. Petter Rudi levelled ten minutes from time for Wednesday. It was like a Dickensian tale of sorts; a ghost of Christmas future was now haunting me after the ghost of Christmas past. Both were named Dalglish.

It seemed like it was the longest preseason ever. I sat moping around at home in Ostrava, fiddling with my thumbs and in general being a miserable bastard. I felt like I was in limbo. I didn't have a club, an agent and didn't know what to do. I was like a zombie wondering around a city of the living dead. It was hard to accept I had left Newcastle United. They had been my life, part of my daily ritual and now it was gone. It was mixed emotions of anger and frustration on a daily basis, yet it was my choice to leave. I could've stayed. I had to snap out of it, refocus and think positively. I had to believe in myself, move on, put the past behind and find another club.

Former Newcastle coach Chris McMenemy, who was acting as an agent at the time, fixed me up with a trial at Wolves. A trial! It was a humbling experience. It was as if the previous eight years at Newcastle had been erased from my CV and I was starting out again. I was part of a team that twice finished runners up in the Premier League and played European football. I trained with the midlands club for a couple of weeks but we couldn't arrange a salary. I was still negotiating my own deals and, despite there being no transfer fee involved, I believed I was being sold short. With no compromise on either side I found myself back in the Czech Republic.

I contacted Banik Ostrava, my old club, to see the lay of the land. The chairman was delighted I'd called and welcomed me back with open arms. He promised he was going to give me this and that, and because I was happy with what he offered, I began training with them ahead of the new season. My old chairman assured me he would arrange a mortgage for a house I'd spotted in Ostrava as part of the deal. My money was tied up in a high interest English bank account and I couldn't get at it without incurring a penalty for taking it out early. The chairman agreed to loan me the money for the house and I was to pay it back in full when I left the club.

I trained with Ostrava believing everything was fine left in our chairman's capable hands. But as it turned out, three months had passed and not a single penny had been deposited in to my bank account. I was informed by the bank a day before the completion date that it hadn't been arranged at all. I had to find the cash or lose the house. The only option I had was taking money from my UK bank account and incurring the commission costs for breaking the deal I entered. I also lost money on changing the currency from English Sterling to Czech Koruna. It was something in the value of £40,000. It was probably foolish of me because I had a gentleman's agreement with the chairman. I didn't sign a contract because we both knew I wouldn't be stopping at the club for any length of time. It was all sorted in the end but I never got a penny in all my time with my former club and I left with a bitter taste in my mouth.

Sheffield Wednesday had made their interest known to me in the autumn and I arrived in south Yorkshire in November of 1998. I met Danny Wilson the manager, with his assistant, Frank Barrow and got a good feeling about my new boss. Danny had just been given the Wednesday job in the summer. He was an Owls old boy, winning the League Cup with them in 1991 and finishing runners up in both the FA Cup and League Cup in 1993. Ironically, Wilson played for Wednesday when I made my debut for Newcastle back in 91. He had taken Barnsley into the Premier League against the odds for the first time in their history. But they only lasted one season in the top flight before being relegated.

Danny was straight talking, open and honest and I thought I could easily work with him. I sat down and discussed my own contract with the manager, chairman and another director. I still didn't have an agent. I felt uncomfortable and knew I was out of my depth when we went in to talk about my contract. I didn't have a club so I was in a bit of a vulnerable position. I wasn't exactly in the best place to negotiate a good deal, and they knew that. I didn't trust any agents after the experiences I'd had in the past but I was still more than happy to control my own destiny rather than it being in someone else's hands.

My mistrust of agents came later in my time at Newcastle. I just accepted what I was offered when I first arrived at St James' Park but I negotiated my second contract on my own with Kevin Keegan, who offered me £2,000 a week. There were the usual bonus rewards for doing well in the cup competitions and league placings but they were never guaranteed. I thought I deserved more but the gaffer said he saw Tommy Wright and I both on equal footing. The club had a wage structure to stick too and so they refused to give me anymore. In essence, he was saying I wasn't the club's number one goalkeeper. I was in a no win situation. I didn't know who to turn too to help negotiate my new deal. If I didn't love the club so much I might have done something drastic. I loved Newcastle and the region. I wanted to stay and so I signed the contract knowing I was worth more than what was being offered.

Paul Stretford got to know about this later on and approached me, saying he would represent me in future contract negotiations. At the time he had a few Newcastle players so I thought maybe he could open discussions with the club and get me a better deal. But when he tried to negotiate my next contract he only managed to get £4,000 a week. I told Stretford it wasn't acceptable because it wasn't much better than my last contract. I told him I could do better by myself, and I did, I sat down with Russell Cushing and I got

£250,000 a year, an extra £50,000 per annum more than he was offering.

There was another guy who got me a two year gloves deal with Sondico, from 1996 to 1998 for £20,000 a year. After a year I still hadn't heard or seen anything of the money I was supposed to get. I would ring the agent every couple of months to find out where it was but never got a reply until 18 months into the deal. When I finally tracked him down he said he didn't know where I was so he couldn't give it to me. Of course he knew where I was. I eventually got the money but is it any wonder I don't trust agents?

There was another occasion when a new shop, Slaters, set up camp in Newcastle and asked me to go down and try on a new line of suits. The Scottish firm took a few photographs and gave me a suit for my troubles. A week later I got a call off a friend saying he had followed a double decker bus in to town and there was a picture of me advertising the menswear shop. I hadn't agreed to do that. And, if I did, surely I should have been rewarded with more than just a new suit. I spoke to the gaffer, Kevin Keegan, about it and he sorted it out for me.

Danny told me I was being brought in as his number one goalkeeper ahead of Wednesday favourite Kevin Pressman. It is all you needed to hear from your boss to give you confidence. It was the first time a manager had said that to me in my career up to that point. The director, however, wanted to keep my wages low but offered a bonus incentive. I didn't know it at the time but the club was in debt. I was obviously suspicious because in the past I have been stung and this was no different. I was offered a three year contract on £4,000 a week, which would have been £192,000 a year. I was to receive £100,000 bonus after I had played 65 games. Yes, I was thinking I'd just rejected a four year contract worth £500,000 a year at Newcastle. Nevertheless, despite selling myself short I was happy I had a club. I was ready to put behind the emotional rollercoaster I'd left at Newcastle and kick start my career.

On my home debut we beat Man United 3-1 at Hillsborough. It was a tremendous result and a great start to my new career in south Yorkshire. A brace from Niclas Alexandersson and a goal from Wim Jonk saw us through. My old team mate Andy Cole netted for the Red Devils. It was a fantastic effort. All the more so when you consider we were only one of three teams to beat Sir Alex Ferguson's side in the league that term, as they won the treble. Likewise, we were only one of four teams to beat runners up Arsenal. It was the infamous game where Paolo Di Canio pushed referee Paul Alcock and got sent off. Di Canio got an 11 match suspension after that assault and I rarely saw him. The incident happened before I arrived at the club and then he was sold to West Ham in the January.

Funny enough, Alcock was in charge when my old team, Newcastle, visited south Yorkshire later that season and had a shocker. I came off my line as Rob Lee went through and I clearly took the ball, but the referee pointed to the spot. Rob apologised but it wasn't his fault. It was the referee. I remember I attempted to take on Shearer in that game with my famous dribble, but he read it. I tried to shake him off but I couldn't because he knew what I was going to do. He'd obviously seen me do it hundreds of times during games and in training. In the end I just had to kick it into the crowd.

We were tipped as one of the favourites to go down at the beginning of the new term but ended the season with the same number of points as Newcastle, 46; but finished above my old side, courtesy of goal difference. We were very much a bit of a yo-yo side. We'd often put a four, five or six game unbeaten run together while on the other hand we could go six games without a win. But when I look back, it was a reasonably good season, overall, and I enjoyed my first campaign in south Yorkshire.

The same couldn't be said of my second season at Wednesday; it turned sour, unfortunately. We started the season poorly, taking just one point from the first nine games before a 5-1 home victory over Wimbledon. Things didn't improve much, Danny Wilson was sacked, in March, and we were eventually relegated, finishing second from bottom.

I started the season in goal but when it looked like we were going down I was being shifted in and out of the team. The Wednesday hierarchy knew that as soon as I hit 65 games for the club they had to pay me £100,000. Once the club were safe in the knowledge I couldn't play 65 games, before the end of my second season, they wanted to put me back in goal. I refused! I thought if this is how you are going to play it then I will play you at your own game. I had a clause in my contract allowing me to move on at the end of my season if I hadn't played those games. Therefore I escaped a third year at the club. There was a bit of fight with the Wednesday chain of command but I got in touch with the FA, who read all of the fine print, and acknowledged I could exercise my right not to take up a third year option. Although I ended the season without a club I wasn't too despondent because the Czech Republic, had qualified for the European Championships, held in Belgium and the Netherlands, and I was the national team number one.

CHAPTER 13
ITALIAN JOB

There were times when I felt like I was an extra in a mafia movie or an action thriller when I lived in Italy. It was like Goodfellas meets Die Hard for a bowl of pasta and a cappuccino in La Dolce Vita. All joking aside, that is probably the best way to describe my Italian adventure. I met people from the mafia; witnessed a web of lies and corruption; extortion; intimidation; drugs; death and, to top it all off, my wife and I had our miracle baby.

I was without a team when I met up with the Czech Republic squad ahead Euro 2000, held in Belgium and Holland, because I didn't take up the option of a third year at Sheffield Wednesday. It was during the championships I met a representative called Zdenek Nehoda. He was a famous Czech agent. He had the likes of Pavel Nedved and Tomas Repka on his books. He approached me and said it would be an honour to have the best goalkeeper in the Czech Republic on his books. I thought to myself, why not, I'll give him a chance. Pavel is a good friend of mine and I hadn't done very well negotiating for myself. Pavel always used to tell me that Lazio were interested in signing me but nothing ever became of it.

After the Euro Championships, my agent and I went to Napoli at first. The Italian club had just been promoted to Serie A and were interested in making me one of their new signings ahead of the new campaign. My wife and I stopped in a hotel ahead of a meeting with the coach, chairman and directors. We were just about to leave the hotel and the doorman stopped us. He told me to leave my watch in the hotel and that my wife shouldn't go out wearing any valuable jewellery because it was too dangerous. He added there was a strong possibility we could get mugged. I was shocked. This was the dawn of a new millennium yet it wasn't safe to walk the streets! I was disgusted. I couldn't walk the streets of Napoli without the danger of being attacked. This was an incredible thought.

The bad impression I had initially formed was soon erased, however, when we went out for dinner to a fantastic seafood restaurant. We stopped there until 3am in the morning. The moon reflected off the water; a warm breeze lapped against the bay; food was delicious and the ambience was serene. I thought it was perfect. After my initial uncertainties, I was thinking maybe this could work.

The Napoli manager was a Czech guy called Zdenek Zeman, who moved to Italy in 1968 and eventually received Italian citizenship. He had a powerful CV, managing Lazio, Roma and Red Star Belgrade, among several others. He contacted my agent and also spoke with me while I was in Belgium for Euro 2000. We had arranged to meet at 10am the following day to thrash out a deal. Three hours had passed and there was no sign of anyone. Just as I said 'that is it, I'm leaving', Zeman and the Napoli secretary turned up. They apologised profusely and made their excuses so I gave them a chance to redeem themselves. But things went from bad to worse.

In the contract negotiations, Zeman said, 'I've seen your cars and the photos of your big house, why do you need so much money?' I was staggered by the question. I thought what business of his was it that I could enjoy a nice car and house, so I simply said, 'I need a decent contract to pay for them.' Zeman then started procrastinating so I just said, 'Forget it. I have been waiting here for three hours and I can see it was for nothing. I'm not going to be insulted by you anymore.' And with that I stood up and left the office. The annoying aspect of this was that we had already agreed what contract I was getting prior to the meeting. The appointment was supposed to be the mere formality of putting my signature on a dotted line.

My agent took a call from Brescia while we were at Milan Airport so, instead of heading home, we flew to the Lombardy region, which was only an hour or so away. We got out at the airport and a car was waiting to take me to the club.

It was while we were negotiating my contract with Brescia that I became aware of Italian football's reputation for corruption. It is rancid the way some Italian clubs conduct their business. The contract I was offered involved half my wages on the record and half my salary off the record because they were trying to save money on paying tax. But my agent and I wanted to do everything legal so instead, Brescia compromised and paid my agent's company half my salary. My agent then paid me half my wages while I got the other half from the club. It was mind boggling. The web of deceit weaved by Brescia came to a climax in the last year of my contract when I didn't get my signing on bonus. It was supposed to go to my agent who was then supposed to pass it on to me.

Six months before the end of my contract, my agent let me know Brescia wanted me to go out on loan to Cosenza. Obviously, I didn't want to go because not only did Brescia owe me a lot of money but I would be hundreds of miles away from my family. Geographically, Cosenza is located in the boot of Italy. The chairman made it known he would pay all the money he owed me if I went. If I didn't go, I wouldn't see a penny of what they owed me. I had a dilemma. But because the club owed me a small fortune in wages I was left with no other option than to go, while Cosenza agreed to pay me for the last six months of my contract.

The day I set off to Cosenza, the chairman fulfilled his promise, but he paid half to my agent and half to me. My agent then let me know Brescia hadn't paid him a penny for negotiating the deal so informed me he was keeping this half of my signing on fee bonus, which was the £170,000. There was little I could do because we had an agreement that half the money went through his firm. There wasn't a problem in the first year. He gave me my bonus from the club. Had I known this was going to happen I wouldn't have gone to Cosenza. The agent, obviously, helped persuade me to go because he knew he would get this money. I felt betrayed because he was supposed to be one of my best friends. In the end he denied Brescia paid him any money, yet I have a receipt slip of the payment. He is still working as an agent in the Czech Republic and now, when we meet, it is very frosty, we never swap anything more than a hello.

I went and played for Cosenza in their battle to stay in Serie B; which failed. They were relegated. In those six months at the club I never got paid a penny. Not only that but the chairman was imprisoned for corruption and all of his assets were seized. That included his houses, cars and the hotel he owned, where most of us were living. In one year, between Brescia's double dealings and Cosenza's deception, I lost £400,000. I couldn't get the money Cosenza owed me because they went bankrupt, cleared their debts and reformed under a different name. I approached the Italian FA about my problem but they said they couldn't do anything about it.

Life as a footballer in Brescia was just as bizarre or surreal. As I said, it was like living in a gangster movie. We weren't having the best of times on the field. I made my debut in a monsoon. The game should never have been played. We lost 4-2 at Udinese. We followed that up with a goalless draw in my home debut before drawing 1-1 away at Fiorentina. We didn't record a win until my eighth game on Italian soil, a 3-0 victory at Reggina.

After the sluggish start, thanks to an unbeaten run in the last 12 games of the campaign, we went on to finish seventh in Serie A, the highest position in the club's history. The catalyst for our successful season was undoubtedly the signing of Roberto Baggio, who had decided not to renew his contract at Inter Milan. Baggio had interest from Barcelona as well but decided to stay in Italy. The Divine Ponytail was joined by Andrea Pirlo from Inter and with, Dario Hubna, they dovetailed beautifully on the pitch.

Pirlo began his career at Brescia. He was the local lad made good and eventually got a big move to Inter Milan before signing for AC Milan. At 16, he was the youngest player ever to play for Brescia. Pirlo got loaned back to Brescia at this time and you could see the skill and potential, what a fantastic player.

Although we also got to the final of the Intertoto Cup, losing on away goals, we never hit the heights of the previous season and just escaped relegation. By this time Hubner had moved on and was replaced by Luca Toni, while Pirlo's place was taken by Barcelona legend Pep Guardiola. The club could afford the likes of Baggio and Guardiola, because it managed to get private sponsorship for them both. The chairman was rich but not mega rich in a Roman Abramovich way. Baggio and Guardiola were at the end of their careers so they wouldn't have been commanding the salaries they had demanded when they were in their pomp. Luca Toni was a young star in the making at Brescia. He was often sent out on loan to give him experience. He never pulled up any trees for us but he did go on to have a fine career and was eventually capped by Italy.

The Brescian locals were more than restless when we failed to record a victory at the start of the 2000-01 season. I remember the hullabaloo after Newcastle lost 1-0 at home to Sheffield United in 2006, when Glenn Roeder was in charge. Newcastle fans made their feelings known they were not happy. Thousands of supporters flocked to the St James' Park entrance doors to voice their opinion. At Brescia, one day, about 30 to 40 of our hardcore supporters came down to the training ground with big sticks, bottles and bricks and were going to sort us out. I remember stepping outside and one of the fans started shouting abuse at me. Calling me a 'foreign bastard', accused me of 'taking money out of the club' and that I was 'a shit goalie'. It was like I had been transported back to St James' Park in 1991! This abuse came after a 2-2 draw at home with Lecce.

There was only one security guard to protect me but I knew I was OK. The supporters gave him total respect because he, and his partner, were in the Italian Secret Service. One of them was like Jean-Claude Van Damme, Bruce Willis and Jackie Chan all in one. I've never seen anything like it. At an AC Milan game the fans were causing trouble and one of them just went in among the supporters like a whirling dervish, wind milling his way through the lot of them. Not one supporter touched him. He moved that fast you couldn't see his hands. It's not as if he was a big giant of a guy. He was about 5ft 10 and of slim build. It's not as if the Brescia followers were fighting with Milan fans, they weren't. They were fighting among themselves. The Brescia supporters were split into two factions when I was there. One set of fans hated the chairman while the other loved him. Both of our security guards generally controlled about 200 of our hardcore supporters when we played away from home.

I remember looking forward to making my home debut for Brescia but 20 minutes into the match the referee stopped it because our supporters were fighting among themselves. Apparently half of the supporters, who backed the chairman, got discounted tickets, while the other half had to pay full price and that is why they were fighting. There were only between 3,000 to 5,000 supporters who came to our home games. We had as many as that coming to watch us train at Newcastle in the early days of my career.

If having your life threatened by supporters wasn't enough, one of our players was connected to the Mafia and carried a gun. He was later banned for life for having drugs in his system. The chairman sent him to the USA for a special medical to see whether he had any banned substances in his body, because he had already been forbidden for playing for drug taking while turning out for one of his former clubs. He had previously been excluded for a season after cocaine was found in his urine sample. We didn't know any of this until later. He was complaining of a stomach ache and just thought he was away to get specialist treatment to resolve the issue. But later on he was banned for life for what was his third offence.

One of our players had his BMW stolen and this guy told the victim he had taken a call from someone who let it be known he could have his car back if he handed over 10,000 Euros. The player says it was OK, the thieves can keep the car because it was insured. This player wasn't involved in the incident but he just knew the people who did it. I was thinking whether my car would be stolen and what would I do if I was in that situation. I checked to see my insurance was up to date when I got home from training that day, I can tell you.

The day the fans came to the training ground looking to sort us out, he took out his gun, laid it on the bench and said 'any of you boys touch me I will shoot you!' I'm sure he didn't have a license to carry a gun. Needless to say no one touched him. At first this episode unnerved me, as well as several other incidents like it. Corruption is rife in Italy from the top to the bottom, but after three years, you get used to it. I got on well with the player as it happened. He seemed like a good guy.

Living in Italy was a bit of a paradox. I wanted to leave yet the lifestyle was fantastic. In a perfect world the Italian way of life and English football would be a match made in heaven. I didn't live in Brescia because it wasn't a very nice place to stay. But I met a guy when I first moved over there who had a jeweller's shop, and he showed me around. I finally found a dream house at Desenzano, in Lake Garda. It was beautiful and I fell in love with it. The only downside was that I was about 50 miles away from Brescia. Then I had to take Vendy to school which was 50 miles further away, so altogether I was doing 100 miles a day. Cost me a fortune in petrol.

One of the saddest moments of my career happened in Brescia when a friend and team mate of mine, Vittorio Mero, died in a car accident on the A4 highway near Rovato. It was a tragedy. Sometimes fate gets in the way when things like this happen. If he hadn't received a yellow card in one of his last games for us he would still be alive today. The card he got meant he was suspended for our next game against Parma. And because Mero wasn't involved with the team he went to training that morning with the other squad members. He was supposed to have lunch with the lads after training but changed his mind, saying he would eat at home and then watch our match on television. If only he hadn't got that yellow card or decided to have lunch with the players, he would still be alive. Within five minutes of leaving the training ground his Polo car had been dragged under a lorry and he was killed. The lorry driver dragged the car for 50 miles before the police stopped him. The driver didn't know. Apparently the lorry driver was overtaking and when he crossed back over into the inside lane he dragged Mero's car fatally under.

Mero's coffin was placed in our gym for five days so we could pay our respects to him. The whole city went to his funeral. I've never witnessed anything like it. I'd never seen how a community can come together as one in grief. It was an uplifting experience in this time of sorrow. Baggio and I were two of the players who carried the coffin. Roberto sat next to me and cried like a baby. He kept asking for more and more handkerchiefs as the service went on. I've never seen anyone as upset as he was. It was bizarre when you think about it because Mero got more respect when he was dead than when he was alive. The club and players all got together and collected 1m Euros for his two-year old boy to collect on his 18th birthday. With all the interest gathered the amount must now be close to 1.5m Euros. Brescia honoured Mero by retiring the number 13 jersey.

But if Mero's death was the most lamentable time of my stay in Italy then the birth of my son was the happiest. There is a common saying that with every death there is a new life and this was certainly the case for me and my wife. Pavla had miscarried with twins when we were first married in Ostrava. This was before we had our first child, Vendy. There was a hell of a mess from her bleeding. I didn't know it at the time but I accidently put the dead foetus of our child down the toilet when I was cleaning her up. I phoned the hospital and they told me to bring in both Pavla and the foetus, but by that time it was too late.

We didn't know she was carrying twins at the time and neither did the hospital. There was still one healthy baby inside my wife. They gave her an injection, some drugs to make her better and cleaned her up. They kept her under observation for three days. But a week after she came home from hospital Pavla fell ill again. This is when we found out she was carrying another baby inside of her. The idiots who gave her the injection in hospital killed the baby. Apparently one of the eggs was ectopic while the other one was growing normally. We were devastated.

We were unaware that one of Pavla's Fallopian tubes had been damaged by the Czech doctors until we were in Italy. Prior to that, we had paid fortunes to have all sorts of fertility treatment, including artificial insemination. None of them had worked. Then the daughter of our chairman was taking with my wife one day and she recommended this doctor in Bologna, who was the top physician in his field in Italy. We called him the Magic Granddad because he was a small guy with silver hair.

Dr Montrucolli was lovely with us and fell in love with our family. He checked out Pavla and found out she had a blocked and damaged Fallopian tube. He managed to operate and open it up. He told us there would be a 20 per cent chance we could conceive inside a year. After that the tube would probably close and our chance would be gone. He gave Pavla some drugs, changed her diet and we were given check-ups every couple of months. There was no artificial insemination involved this time and we could have sex normally. And within seven months of the operation, Pavla was pregnant with a boy, Maxim. It must have cost me half a year's wages, because we went private, but he was worth every penny.

A few months after Maxim was born my wife was sitting watching television one evening. She called me and asked me to ring Dr Montrucolli because she had a strange feeling something was wrong. I was in England at the time but I called him and our worst fears were confirmed. His wife answered the telephone and said he had died of a heart attack. Maxim was the last baby he had delivered. He had planned to go to the USA and use our struggle to have a baby and the procedures used as part of his lecture tour, and his book, because Maxim's birth was a one in a million chance. The only patient his wife had ever come to see was Pavla. Maybe it was because our son was a miracle child, I don't know. But she presented my wife with an angel charm to give to Maxim for good luck.

I remember when I signed for Brescia, Pavel Nedved called me and said you will have a baby. Nedved knew we wanted another child but couldn't have one. Pavel told me that him and his wife had struggled to have a child yet when they moved to Italy, within no time they had two children. I kind of laughed off his suggestion but my Czech teammate was insistent. He said 'I'm not sure whether it is the food, the air or the lifestyle, but you will have more children'. Now I tell everyone to go to Italy if they want to have a baby.

Roberto Baggio wouldn't have been on the megabucks salary he had been on in his pomp but he still would've been the highest paid player at Brescia. As part of his contract he arranged to have a fitness coach, physio and had every Tuesday off. He was an outstanding professional footballer. He was one of the first at training in the morning and he was the last to leave. I was the second last to leave. I'd never known anyone leave training before I did until I met him. He used to warm down and finish with a massage after every session. His body was getting older and he had a few injuries so he had to manage and look after his body better to get the most out of his twilight years.

Roberto converted to Buddhism when he was a teenager after a career-threatening injury looked to have stopped him playing. He used to pray for three to four hours every day. He always got his own room in a hotel when we travelled to away games rather than share like the rest of us. He believed Buddhism helped him to recover faster from ailments. Injuries that were supposed to keep him out of action for four months, took two. He had incredible mental strength and a will to succeed. He scored 45 goals in 95 games for Brescia. Not a bad return rate for someone whose best years were supposed to be behind him. When training was finished he'd stop behind and practice free-kicks with 30 or 40 balls. On a match day, if we got a free kick inside 30 yards he'd score one in every two or three. He still had the skill, vision and class. He was one of the greatest footballers in the world.

Baggio was a good family man. I always used to sing this Czech folk song every day and he picked up on it. He'd say, 'Pav, that has a nice melody.' And he would hum along to it when I sang the song. He was good fun as well. We had this striker called Dario Hubner, who dived over my arm in training to cheat a penalty this one time. I hated anyone cheating at the best of times but this was in training. There was no need for it. There was no money involved, no points and no trophy. I was furious. I went absolutely berserk!

I said, 'I'm going to fucking kill you!' I chased the guy around the pitch for the rest of the session. Hubner kept well away and wouldn't even come in to the changing rooms after the session had finished for a shower. Roberto shouted 'there he is', pointing out where he has was hiding. 'Pav, he's a bad man, look, he's shitting himself.' But that was Roberto, taking the sting out of the situation and eventually we all fell about laughing.

Pep Guardiola arrived in my second season and only played half of it because he tested positive for drugs and got a four month ban, although he was later cleared of any wrong doing. They found nandrolone in his system which is an anabolic steroid, seen by many as a performance enhancing stimulant. I remember he had this special bottle in the dressing room while he was at Brescia. He was drinking from this bottle all of the time. The club doctor asked what was in it. Pep said there was nothing in the drink and told him how he took it when he played at Barcelona.

There were several well known internationals, including, Edgar Davids, who were tested positive for the same drug, nandrolone, around the same time. It was a shock because it didn't sit with the man I knew. He was a good family man who always tried to help people. Despite the wealth of experience and trophies he won, he was a humble down to earth guy. He never played the big superstar or thought he was any better than the other players. I was confident it was a mistake.

Pep was a very clever man, calm and in control. He always offered advice or an opinion to our manager Carlo Mazzone when he was asked. Did I think he was going to go on to be the great manager he is today? He was certainly an intelligent man with a great football brain. It's not a surprise but then I played with a lot of players who were tactically aware and knowledgeable about the game.

I need to see Pep, the more I think about it. He owes me several dinners. We always used to have a side bet in training because we were on opposing sides in the games and his team never beat mine. I've seen him only once since he left Brescia and that was when he was Barcelona manager and was in the Czech Republic for a Champions League game against Victoria Plzen. In the press conference he made a joke that he was pleased I wasn't playing against him because of his struggles to score against me in the past. Yes, I need to speak with Pep and get those dinners he owes me.

CHAPTER 14
POMPEY, PORTUGAL AND BLOWING BUBBLES

Living in a London hotel was convenient because I was only 20 minutes to an airport. The flights to Italy were between £50 and £60. The taxi fare on the other side was more expensive than the flights. But being cooked up in a hotel meant I didn't get the chance to mix with the players at Pompey or West Ham, so there aren't many exciting stories from my time down south. The most interesting moment of that time was on a flight from Gatwick to Milan. I was walking through the terminal this one time and I could see people pushing and whispering. Obviously, I've become quite accustomed to it over the years. People see a familiar face or footballer and it happens all the time, so I thought it was me. Then I realise they're looking beyond me and I see this little tiny fella behind me, no bigger than a dwarf. You might have heard of him. Apparently he's quite big in the film industry and has this fantastic house near Lake Como. George Clooney anyone?

The only other attention-grabbing happening, although it wasn't that interesting to be honest, more bizarre than anything else. I got a taxi to the airport this one time in Italy when I was on my way back to Portsmouth. The cab driver asked whether I was sitting comfortably in my seat, which I was. He kept nodding and winking and laughing. I'm thinking, what's the matter with the twitchy guy? Is he off his trolley? He then told Kevin Costner had just been sitting in the very same seat. I was wondering why he was telling me this. I thought would he tell Kevin Costner the same, Pavel Srnicek had been sitting in the seat prior to him getting in? Give me a break, man. Must be a lonely life as a cab driver if that's the best he could come up with.

I returned to the Premier League and British football for only one season with Portsmouth and West Ham. Pompey, who had just been promoted to the Premier League for the first time, hadn't played in the top flight for about 15 years. My old coach Chris McMenemy arranged the move with, the south coast outfit's manager, Harry Redknapp. I was only brought in as cover for my old mate Shaka Hislop and Harald Wapenaar. Once again, there was no transfer fee involved. I didn't get a signing on fee, only a monthly salary. But I was looking forward to playing at Fratton Park. I remember playing there for Newcastle and the home support was quite vociferous for such a small stadium. The fact my old Czech Republic team mate, Patrik Berger, was there was a deciding factor, while I also knew Dejan Stefanovic from my time at Sheff Wed.

I remember a story Patrick Berger once told me when he was at Liverpool with Vladimir Smicer. Their contracts were both up for renewal and their agent approached them and asked what they were looking for to stay on at the Anfield club. The agent invited them to write on a piece of paper what they wanted and he would negotiate with the club. Berger told me he wrote an astronomical figure for the agent as a piss take; not expecting Liverpool to agree. The agent went away and then came back and said the club had agreed. Berger said it was like winning the lottery. He couldn't believe they gave him the obscene amount of money he asked for.

Harry Redknapp was always great to me, even when I wasn't playing for him. I was back at St James' Park for a trip after I had finished playing this one time. Harry was the visiting Tottenham manager and stopped to give me a hug when he saw me. He said it was great to see me. It was a genuine gesture because he was walking one way and I caught his eye in the distance, so he went out his way to approach me. Harry was always polite and a gentleman. Yet I was only with him at Pompey for a few months. I remember asking when I was there on the south coast whether it would be OK to go home every now and again. He knew my family were in Italy and he was fine with that. He cut me a lot of slack. He was a proper players' manager.

I made my debut for Pompey in a south coast League Cup derby against Southampton which we lost 2-0. I followed that up with a clean sheet in a goalless draw at the Riverside against Middlesbrough. But that was it for me at Portsmouth because I left about a month later to go to West Ham on loan. My old friend from the Czech Republic, Ludo Miklosko, who was the Hammers' goalkeeper coach, got in touch and asked whether I would be interested in coming to Upton Park. He knew I was only at Portsmouth as cover and reckoned I'd have more chance of getting some games in with the east end of London club.

West Ham were in the second tier at that time as they got relegated the previous season. Again, I only made two appearances for the Hammers, against Derby and Crystal Palace, as they tried to regain their top flight status. We lost 1-0 at Selhurst Park while drawing 0-0 at home with the Rams. One of the most memorable incidents came when I was on the bench for the trip to Sunderland. I climbed out of the dug out at the Stadium of Light and went to warm up. The abuse I received was phenomenal. At first I was shocked. I didn't know why, but after a few moments the penny dropped and I enjoyed it. This is what I missed about Premier League football; the passion and excitment. I was a Newcastle favourite so therefore I was a symbol, or figure, of hate for the Mackems. It was funny. I was thinking, if only the supporters knew I nearly signed for them several years previously.

I got on well with Hammers boss Alan Pardew. So that's two managers I had good relationships with. You see, Freddie Fletcher was wrong; I didn't have a problem with every coach I played for. I was at the Boleyn Ground until the end of the season and Alan says there was another year for me if the Hammers beat Crystal Palace in the play off final at Cardiff. Unfortunately Palace won and money was in short supply so I was looking for yet another club.

I really wanted to stay because I had a great relationship with Ludo. We trained well and I know his family. I also knew Tomas Repka from the national team. I think Pardew was happy to have me at West Ham because he thought I could keep Repka in check. The Czech defender was a good player but always got booked, sent off or gave away free kicks in dangerous places around the penalty area. Tomas also wrote a book about his life where he admitted he gave away a penalty in a game playing for Ceske Budejovice against Liberec. Liberec were fighting for the title against Repka's former club, Sparta Prague. Repka had fallen out with the Sparta president Daniel Kretinsky and wanted revenge. He achieved his goal.

After I left West Ham I found myself in a familiar position once again, I was without a football club. Nevertheless, a Portuguese agent got in touch with me and asked whether I would be interested in playing for Beira Mar. I'm not sure if it was the British connection because Mick Wadsworth was the manager, Sir Bobby Robson's former right hand man. But he only took charge of four games before he quit. We had six points from the four games and were only four points off the leaders, Benfica. It was a shame because he was a good guy. I don't know why he left, whether it was for personal or football reasons.

I initially enjoyed my time at Beira Mar. The move all hinged on whether there were any English speaking schools for my daughter Vendy. Fortunately, there was one that met our needs. Being a footballer is hard on your family because you tend to live like a bit of a nomad or gypsy, moving from place to place. But for Vendy, living and going to school in Portugal was the best time of her life. She was 16-years-old at this time and graduated from school. She can now speak English, Czech, Italian, Portuguese and Russian. We took a house on the beach; it was a new challenge in a new cultural environment with a nice climate. The football side wasn't too great because we got relegated from the top flight in my first season but it was a good experience.

It was a poor country, poor club but a fantastic new stadium which was constructed for the 2004 European Championships. Each seat was a different colour to make it look full all of the time, despite it being empty most of the time. On the other hand, the training facilities were very mediocre.

I had the best salary at the club although it still wouldn't compare to a Premier League club. On the other hand, the Brazilian players, were only getting between 1000 and 2000 Euros a month. There is always hundreds of Brazilians living and playing in Portugal because they are cheap, can speak the language and there was always a chance a gem could be unearthed from amongst them. We had seven players from Brazil in the first team and the dressing room was one of the best I had ever been in. The spirit was fantastic and they were all good fun. There never seemed to be any problems with them. They never complained and they were always singing and dancing. We often went out to eat and they would go mad for their beans, Feijao. They would say, 'Come and eat with us, Pav. Eat the Feijao. It is fantastic.' I would go, 'Boys, do you not eat anything else?' And they would reply, 'You should taste my mother's beans.' And I'm thinking, that doesn't sound appropriate, no thanks boys. We would eat in a, kind of a, food court in a supermarket. They used to have something similar in the Monument, Newcastle city centre, and the Metro Centre. And they would be singing, dancing and laughing, while they ate. It was extraordinary. It didn't matter, forgive the pun, that they didn't have two beans to rub together. They were having a good time and a great bunch of lads.

After Mick left we got this coach, Manuel Cajuda, who would come in every day and just talk, what would seem like hours. He loved listening to himself. And they were spectacularly boring dialogues. He could talk a proverbial glass eye to sleep. The players knew I had to undertake a 100 mile round trip every morning to get to training and I regularly nodded off to sleep while he was blathering on. The players would be nudging each other, sniggering and whispering, 'Look at Pav.' I would snap out of it and then a few moments later I would be off again. He had the perfect voice to cure insomnia.

The training sessions were not only poor, as in they were far too easy, they were boring as well. Beira Mar's other goalkeeper, Paulo Sergio, agreed with me. They were easily the worst coaching sessions I'd experienced in my life as a professional. One day I'd had enough of his boring monotone; why we were in the shit at the bottom of the league and what we could do to get out of it. So I stood up and said to the Cajuda, 'If you excuse me boss. I am the most experienced player in the squad and I've played all over the world. If you let me, I'll explain why I think we're struggling.' I then told him we didn't train properly, there was no structure and we are physically unfit. He listened for a while, contemplated and then we all went out to train.

Cajuda changed a few things but the session was still easy. At the end of training Cajuda and the goalkeeper coach approached me. I can't remember the goalkeeping coach's name, although he was one of the biggest back-stabbers I've ever come across in football. He got Paulo Sergio and I together and said, 'We don't train properly, eh? I'll show you what proper training is.' The bastard might as well of nailed us to a cross and flogged us. He had us running and doing shuttles from one end of the six yard box to the other until we were physically sick. I saw the goalkeeping coach laughing as we collapsed, exhausted. I thought he shouldn't be laughing.

Paulo and I had to crawl on our hands and knees to the changing room. We lay on the floor and benches for ages before we could summon enough strength to take a shower. I thought I was going to die. It was a horrible experience. I wasn't a young man back then, I was 36. The session finished at 7pm, we left the training ground at 9pm. Ask anyone I have ever played with and they will tell you I was one of the fittest around. But this nearly killed me. I have to give credit to Paulo. He stuck by me and didn't quit and he could have. It was my big mouth, if you like, and my punishment. Soon after this episode, Cajuda went to the chairman and tried to get me thrown out of the club. But in the end it was him who got sacked. He lasted ten games in Averio.

Augusto Inatio was a different kettle of fish altogether. He was a good coach. He knew I was experienced and just wanted me fit and ready for Saturdays when we played. He allowed me to set up my own goalkeeping sessions to prepare for the game. It worked a treat.

We bounced back from relegation to win the league by four clear points from Aves, losing only twice in the process. I was named the club's player of the year which was a fitting end to a successful campaign. Unfortunately, Beira Mar couldn't afford to pay me so my Portuguese adventure was over after only two seasons. They were struggling to pay my wages in my second term and when I left they had to come to some agreement to settle their debt.

CHAPTER 15
COUNTRY CALLS

My international career resembled my domestic career in a lot of respects, as in it raised more questions than provided answers. It was very much a case of, what if? What if Newcastle had won the Premier League title in 1996? What if the Czech Republic had beaten Germany in the 1996 European Championships? It would have changed my life forever, of course. Instead, losing both the Premier League title and the Euro 96 final, in the same calendar year, kind of symbolises my life and career; one of disappointment. It was always a case of so near, yet so far.

I won 49 caps playing for my country and kept 23 clean sheets. It would've been closer to 100 if it was not for Petr Kouba. But, then again, maybe I would've won less international honours had Kouba been a regular for Deportivo La Coruna. My friend and colleague left Sparta Prague after Euro 96 for the Spanish outfit but rarely played. Deportivo manager John Toshack did not rate him. And the way the Czech Republic national football team operates, you had to be playing for your club otherwise you wouldn't be picked to play. I suppose Kouba's adversity was my good fortune. It was a shame because he was a fantastic goalkeeper.

Former Czech manager, Václav Ježek, was made aware that I was playing in the Premier League for Newcastle and decided to visit me on Tyneside. How it had escaped the notice of the Czech Republic's international set up is a mystery. Nevertheless, he came to watch me play in a game at St James' Park. We went out to dinner later that evening after the match. He couldn't believe it was possible that I had been in the North-East for a few years yet no one in the Czech FA knew about me or how well I was playing. Ježek was even more surprised considering we were one of the best teams in the Premier League. All the same, I was called into the squad for a World Cup qualifier at Wales in 1993. We were still called Czechoslovakia at the time, and most of the group was made up from the old regime. I was the second choice goalkeeper for the 2-2 draw at Cardiff Arms Park. It wasn't until over a year later that I actually made my debut for the Czech Republic at the age of 26 in a European qualifier against Malta.

My international career started well with a clean sheet against the Maltese in a 0-0 draw. It was a bad result for us. We missed a penalty but should've won. We had loads of chances. Admittedly, I had little to do. Then I recorded a second consecutive clean sheet in Holland, in another 0-0 draw, which was pleasing. I always seemed to play well against the Netherlands. I remember there was a Czech agent, called Pavel Paska in the bar after the game, who had followed my career with interest. We were chatting and he commented how remarkable my story was. He also congratulated me on my achievements: coming from a tiny village in Bohumín, without any help, yet becoming a footballer on the international stage. He added the odds of that happening were astronomical.

The way my international career ended was a big disappointment but that seemed to be the story of my life. Karel Bruckner took hold of the reins when Jozef

Chonanec stepped down after we failed to qualify for the 2002 World Cup. Bruckner was Chonanec's assistant so he was always involved with the squad. Despite his spiteful refusal to pick me for the under-21s, several years earlier, we got on well. He knew I was stuck on 49 caps, after we didn't make progress beyond the European group stage for the tournament held in South Korea and Japan, following our two-legged defeat to Belgium in the play-offs. But he casually mentioned that I deserved to win a 50th cap when we were chatting soon after the loss.

The new campaign had kicked off and it wasn't long before the first international break was upon us. I wondered whether I would get a call, like Bruckner promised. Sure enough, prior to the first fixture of the new international season, I saw there was a missed call on my mobile phone from the new Czech boss. It looked like as if he was going to honour that discussion and I was going to get that 50th cap after all. I have to admit, I was excited when I returned Bruckner's call. I shouldn't have been. Bruckner had only bad news. He told me he rang my number by mistake. I was devastated. How can you possibly do that? He never called me again. I felt like shit.

Why was I never called up again? Maybe Bruckner was under pressure from the press and media and supporters. I had been chosen to represent my country when I was in between clubs. I was also selected when I had a knee injury. Some people thought the other goalkeepers underneath me should be given a chance. We had a promising young keeper called Petr Cech. There was a rally to get the 20-year-old in the team before he was ready, I felt. But I was only 32 and still young enough to win more caps.

After a first leg play off in Brussels, against Belgium in 2001, which we lost 1-0, Pavel Nedved, Karel Poborsky, Patrik Berger and I got our heads together and decided we weren't go to say anything to the press because they were giving us loads of shit. The press would be asking one of our tennis players, golf players or ice hockey players who they thought should be in the Czech Republic football team. It was madness. It would be the same if they asked me about golf, tennis or ice hockey, I wouldn't have a clue. It got that bad my wife was getting grief in Ostrava. Pavla pleaded with me to quit the team before the second leg in Prague because of the hassle. I got so sick I told one reporter to 'go and ask the gypsies who should be in the team?' It obviously didn't go down well and the press went after me, despite playing well in both legs.

We were under a lot of pressure for the second leg after losing the first contest to a Gert Verheyen strike. Our cause wasn't helped by Tomas Repka seeing red just before half time. A contentious Marc Wilmots penalty four minutes from the end ensured the Red Devils would go through. The referee Anders Frisk was abysmal. We should have had at least one penalty. A few years later, Frisk got hit by a coin at AS Roma. I thought that was karma paying him a visit for performing like a clown in one of the most important games of my international career. After the match I confronted Belgium national coach Robert Waseige because he was laughing at me as I was walking off the pitch. I was furious and stormed down the tunnel and kicked in Frisk's door, in the referee's room. The

UEFA delegate witnessed the incident and I got fined 2,000 Swiss francs.

The following day the press wrote I had attacked the Belgium coach. All I did was swear at him for laughing at me. It was an outrageous accusation. Waseige was a 60 year-old man. There was no mention of the door being kicked in. It was no surprise to see controversy surrounding Frisk in a Champions League tie between Chelsea and Bayern Munich a few years later. Football is a better place without him in the middle causing a storm. This was another sad chapter in my life. I never played in any World Cup finals. The paradox to all of this is that we were ranked second and third in the world during my playing career. Despite this, it was one of the greatest Czech teams in its history.

I may have played every game of Euro 2000 in Belgium and Holland but the highlight of my international career was, undoubtedly, Euro 96, despite never kicking a ball in anger. My coach, and hero, Ivo Viktor, told me after the championships in England had finished, that the manager, Dusan Uhrin, and the coaching staff considered playing me in the final. I often think if I'd got a break like that it would've changed my life.

Euro 96 was special for the Czech squad because we built a cocoon around our base in the hotel. We even had Czech beer sent to us. We lost 2-0 to Germany in our first game and everyone was tipping us for an early exit. We then beat Italy 2-1 in our second group game. The Italians made several changes for the match after beating Russia 2-1 in their curtain raiser because they thought we were rubbish. We drew

3-3 against Russia in our final group game while the German keeper Kopke saved a Gianfranco Zola penalty and we got through to the knock out stages.

After our last group game we could feel the confidence and spirit lift in the camp. We started to gain some momentum after that and beat Portugal 1-0 in the quarter finals before disposing of France on penalties in the semi-final after a 0-0 draw. I was probably enjoying it because the tournament was in England and I felt like I was at home. Like the 1976 champions, 20 years earlier, we were a team of unknowns. Maybe Berger and Pavel Kuka were known, but no one else. After the competition Poborsky went to Man United, Nedved to Lazio and Berger and Vladimir Smicer to Liverpool.

As a child growing up in Czechoslovakia there was never any Czech football on the television. The only football we had on TV was Serie A in Italy. Although when the big tournaments came around every two years we used to get the World Cup or European Championships. And like everyone else I used to follow our national team. We always used to have a good selection of goalkeepers to choose from, in what are now Czech and Slovakia states.

My sporting hero was Ivo Viktor. He played for Czechoslovakia between 1966 and 1977 and is the country's most celebrated goalkeeper. He was the hero of the 1976 European Championship final when we beat West Germany 5-3 on penalties when the contest finished 2-2 after extra time. In the same year he was third behind Franz Beckenbaur and Rob Rensenbrink, from Anderlecht, in the European Footballer of the year award. He was the country's player of the year five times.

He played most of his career at Dukla Prague and when I joined the army to do my national service, who is my coach? Ivo Vikto, my hero! He, of course, later became the national team coach and therefore I got to play under him again. We had, and still have a great relationship to this day. It gave me an enormous amount of confidence to know, one of the greatest players in Czech history, if not the greatest, had faith in me as a goalkeeper.

Vikto was brave, fast and could throw the ball well over the halfway line. And that was in the days with the old heavy footballs. If I had a day off and the team was short of a goalkeeper, he would go in goal, even when he was supposed to be too old to play. My fellow goalkeepers and I were often embarrassed because of how good he was, in his mid 50s. This was about the time of the Euro 96 Championships. I would still go and watch the sessions and think how fantastic he was. And he was still brave, diving at the feet of players and going up for challenges with players half his age. He wouldn't grumble, he would just get on with it. He had a son who was a goalkeeper too but it was tough for him standing in the shadow of his father. I feel sorry for those kids who have a famous sportsman or woman as their parents. He packed in playing because he just couldn't compete with his father, which was unfair. If he had a choice who to put in goal, he would always choose me. And today I still have a very good relationship with him.

One of the biggest compliments or endorsements he gave to me was a book he had written. It was a small book of about 90 pages and it was all to do with being a goalkeeper. He said 'Pavel, I have written the first part of the book and now it is your turn to write part two. This was around the time I first started to play for the national team in 1994. He used to take a coaching session on one day and then he would ask me to take training because he was confident in the knowledge I had learned despite my young years. It was like he was the master and I was his apprentice, like Obi wan Kenobi and Luke Skywalker.

I remember the 1976 final against West Germany very well. My family and I watched it on the television. We only had four channels and, because we were living in a Communist country, the news was all propaganda. You didn't really know what was happening in the outside world. But this was a good sporting event so the powers that be let the country watch the football. I know Communism wasn't a good thing but at least we got to play every sport. We were made to try every sport but I loved that. Now it seems you pick one sport, such as tennis, and concentrate on that one discipline. Football was my number one priority but I still played another ten different sports. I know we didn't have the distractions youngsters have now with computers, iPads and mobile phones, we didn't even have a landline telephone when I was a kid.

But I remember the 1976 final as if it was only yesterday. It was a hot summer evening and everyone had their windows open. You could hear all the shouting, screaming and cheering from all around. And the penalty shoot out, Panenka's chip, wow, it was amazing. Panenka is a legend because of that penalty.

And the Czech commentator, Karol Polak, when Panenka scored was hilarious. His voice went extraordinarily higher than usual. We all still chuckle about it today. He is the Czech version of the British commentator Kenneth Wolstenholme, who coined the phrase: They Think it's All Over!

Ivo Vikto once told me about the second goal he conceded in the final, when West Germany equalised two minutes from time to take the tie into extra time. He came to get the cross and he missed it. He says, 'No-one remembers that I was probably the best goalkeeper in the tournament and had a great game in the final. They all remember that mistake.' So he told me never to worry about making an error. He said goalkeepers will always be remembered for gaffs more than great saves. It was the same when Olivier Bierhoff's shot was mishandled by Kouba, against Germany in 1996 final. It is remembered because it was not only a blunder but also the first Golden Goal in the history of the competition. Nobody remembers anything else about Kouba, which is sad. Outfield players can get away with mistakes all of the time. It is different for us. It is highlighted and magnified beyond reason.

After Ivo Vikto, Michel Preud'homme was the goalkeeper I admired the most. I first come across him in the early 1980s when Belgium had an excellent international football team. I liked his style of goalkeeping and how he looked. He was considered one of the world's best keepers during his career. He made incredible saves, great agility and reflexes. He was the first winner of the Yashin Award for being the best shot stopper at the 1994 World Cup. The award was named after Lev Yashin, who is credited as being one of the greatest keepers that ever lived. I feel Preud'homme was a modern great. It was just a shame his career was tainted somewhat by a scandal involving his former team Standard Liege in the 1980s. My Newcastle team mate Philippe Albert told me several players in the Standard side were implicated in fixing a match against Thor Waterschei, to allow them to win the league, in what became known as the Standard-Waterschei Affair. Preud'homme and several of his other teammates received lengthy bans.

I didn't have many sporting heroes apart from Viktor, Preud'homme and Ivan Lendl. The Czech tennis player is also from Ostrava. I think his parents still live there. I have never met him. He has visited several times but I have never been able to meet up with him. I've always been called away or working when he has been in the Czech Republic.

I admired his will to win and determination. I have heard stories about how he would reduce himself to tears to push himself through the pain barrier. He probably wasn't the best technical player, like a John McEnroe, but he had resolve, purpose and the strength of mind to succeed. He was always dignified when he was being interviewed. He was never disparaging about people on TV. I don't think it's a coincidence Andy Murray had most of his success when Lendl was his coach. He was never one for small talk and I don't think I ever saw him angry on the tennis court. This is what I liked about him. He also had a gruelling training schedule when he was at the top of his game. I have always been wary of meeting Ivan because there is that saying that you shouldn't meet your heroes because they will disappoint you; although that didn't happen with Ivo Viktor.

A teacher at my school used to train with Ivan Lendl when he was a boy, and teenager, and often spoke about his hard work and dedication. She said it was hard to get him off the tennis court. He wanted to play as long as there was light or daylight. There were times where he used to cry because he couldn't get a routine right. And rather than quit, he would stop out until he mastered the technique. I always felt I had this connection with him because he was from Ostrava. I loved his attitude; will to win and the 100 per cent he put in to his sport. I would like to think I applied myself in the same way.

I remember the 1982 World Cup, in Spain, where we had two 1-1 draws with France and Kuiwait while losing 2-0 to England. Panenka, the hero of 1976 scored both our goals. In Italia, 1990, we lost in the quarter finals to Germany, courtesy of a Lothar Matthaus penalty. We won two games in the group stages before losing to the hosts Italy 2-0. We then beat Costa Rica, conquerors of Scotland, 4-1. Tomas Skuhravy netted a hat-trick in that match. Skuhravy got a transfer to Genoa after the World Cup. He scored five goals and was the second top scorer in the competition. I remember when I got called into the squad for the first time, in the qualifier against Wales, in 1993, Skuhravy arrived in a private jet. He turned up smoking a cigar and wearing dark Ray Bans sunglasses. It was quite extraordinary to see the change in a guy, who was from ordinary humble origins, turn up like a superstar. I was like a rabbit caught in the headlights. I was playing at Newcastle with a lot of established footballers, most of them internationals, but none of them behaved like a big time Charlie.

I have been told that in Kevin Keegan's autobiography he said Shaka Hislop and I were very good goalkeepers, but not great ones. How many people are great at their jobs? On the other hand, how many people can say they are very good at their jobs? There is a fine line between the both. Maybe had I won the title at Newcastle or played in goal for the Czech Republic and won a trophy people would've said I was great. How many footballers have won the Champions League, who weren't regarded as a great player yet have been awarded the highest European honour for a domestic team? I know it's a hypothetical question. I might not have been the best goalkeeper in the world but I was honest and never cheated. I can look in the mirror every day and say I gave my best. That's all I could do. If that isn't good enough in the eyes of some critics then that's life, I can't change that.

CHAPTER 16
TESTIMONIAL

Steve Harper's testimonial was the last time all the lads from Entertainers' era got together. I have to say, it was an outstanding occasion. For selfish reasons, to play again at St James' Park against AC Milan in front of a full house was extraordinary. But it was a fitting tribute to a fantastic servant to Newcastle United. For most of the time Steve played second fiddle to Shay Given and yet he remained loyal to the club. He could've left and had a great career somewhere else and, who knows, even played for England.

I met Steve Harper when he was just 15-years-old and a junior at the club. We got on really well right from the off and became lifelong friends. At first I wasn't sure whether he wanted to be a footballer or whether he was going to make it. It wasn't a lack of talent holding him back because it was apparent he was a fine goalkeeper. He had all the attributes to become a very good goalkeeper. But it didn't seem as if he was completely focused on football. It appeared football was only a second interest to him. He was a very good cricketer, you see, and I felt his career lay in that direction. Maybe he was confused and keeping his options open.

Later on, as he developed into a young man and a wonderful goalkeeper, he was sent on loan to Hartlepool and Huddersfield, where he earned glowing reports. It was around this time that I left the club but we always stayed in touch and I always kept a keen eye on his career.

Steve stepped in several times as cover for Shay Given and never let the side down. There was even talk of an England call when he had established himself. I think it would've been deserved because he was as good, if not better, than those who were being called up at the time. Should he have left to further his career? Probably, yes. But he is a Geordie lad and he loved his home-town club. You have to give Steve credit for remaining loyal to United. It would've been easy for him to leave Tyneside. It seems the club has been in a perpetual state of political turmoil since I left in 1998. Many would've bailed out long before he was eventually let go. Yet he stuck with the club through thin and thin and fought for the number one shirt.

Steve was rewarded for his loyalty and service to the club and eventually broke my record for the most clean sheets in a season, when United were promoted back to the Premier League. I couldn't have been happier for him. When Steve got in touch with me to come and play in his testimonial it was a privilege and an honour. I approached Steve in the lounge after the game to tell him how much I enjoyed it and to wish him all the best. He got up and gave me a hug and said that if it wasn't for me he wouldn't have been a goalkeeper. It made me feel fantastic. Steve is very much in my heart. I subsequently read a newspaper article, where he made it known he wants to help others in the game because that is what I did with him when he was a kid. I felt honoured when I read that.

It was a shame but there was one incident that soured the day for me. No, it wasn't Paolo Di Canio scoring from the penalty spot. My long time friend from Newcastle, Lorenzo was a big fan of Franco Baresi. The former Italy captain, and legend, was his hero. Baresi played for AC Milan that night and after the game Lorenzo asked whether I could get his autograph. I thought that, with me, being a player it would be no problem. We had shaken hands on the pitch after all. So in the lounge, after the game, I approached him, spoke in Italian and asked for an autograph. He didn't even look at me, just waved his hand in the air, saying he had no time and walked away. I was astonished and it made my blood boil. I was going to go after him but Lorenzo pulled my arm and told me just to leave it. What a miserable bastard.

Baresi was a great player. One of the greatest players of his generation and maybe one of the best defenders Italy has ever produced. He has won the World Cup; European Champions League titles and countless domestic trophies. Yet, now, I have no respect for the man. I thought, what a shit! This was a classic case that you should never meet your heroes because of their tendency to let you down. This was no more personified than in this example.

Peter Beardsley's testimonial was another great night. I hadn't been gone a season when Pedro had his benefit match. We played against Celtic, who were his favourite side, after Newcastle of course. I remember running towards the Gallowgate End to warm up and the fans started cheering for me. When we got back into the dressing room after the game, one of the lads said, 'Fucking hell, Pav, we thought it was your testimonial!' I says, 'Come on boys, give me a break.' It's not until you leave you realise how much you miss

St James' Park. I maybe took it for granted a little bit at the time.

I don't think anyone missed Pedro's testimonial. Even Kenny Dalglish had been invited and Pedro wasn't a big fan of his. Dalglish had been sacked at the beginning of that season, while I was playing in goal for Sheffield Wednesday. But we were all civil towards the ones we didn't particularly care for and genuinely pleased to see the old boys. These occasions are always great to see one another because there is always one of the lads who is ten kilos bigger, so you get to take the piss.

I had met Gazza before Pedro's special day but it was great to see him. It is sad what has happened to him because he is a lovely guy. I met him when I was out with the Newcastle lads in a bar in the town back in the 1990s. It was like he was my best friend. He was like, 'How are you doing Pav, you OK?' I was thinking, Gazza knows me? He is a good lad. I hope he can pull himself through these tough times.

The third time I was back for a benefit game was for the Entertainers' match. I had mixed feelings about it when it was first suggested because the Liverpool game at Anfield in 1996 wasn't a favourite memory of my time at Newcastle. In fact it was the single worst moment of my spell at the club. Time is a great healer, however, and I suppose I could maybe exorcise the ghosts of Anfield. But then you put all of those bad memories to the back of your mind and think, it would be great to see all of the lads again.

Steve Wraith, a former fanzine writer and now a promoter, among several other things, got in touch with me a year before it was actually staged and pitched the idea. There were problems before we got started. First Steve didn't get on with the owner Mike Ashley, while Kevin Keegan said he would never go to St James' Park until Ashley had left the club. I know Steve, and the organisers, tried to get St James' Park but because Keegan was involved, I'm guessing Ashley wouldn't allow it. Then it was going to be played at Darlington before the plug was pulled on it and it was eventually staged at Kingston Park. There was a full house of maybe 10,000 to 12,000 fans. I would imagine they could've filled St James' Park but it wasn't to be.

Steve has to be congratulated for pulling this altogether. I needed notice and permission, to get away for a couple of days from my job at Sparta Prague. Tino travelled over 13,000 miles to play in the match. A lot of players had other commitments yet still made the effort to be there. The only player missing was Peter Beardsley. It was a shame Pedro wasn't there because he was a fans' favourite on both sides. I don't know the politics but it was probably because he works for the club and wasn't allowed to play. I don't know. Pedro was like the right-hand man of Kevin. Keegan loved him like a son in the same way he loved Rob Lee and Alan Shearer. Pedro acted like a buffer between the manager and the players at St James' Park when he returned in 1993.

Shearer just cracks me up every time I see him. I conceded one goal where, I think it was, Terry Mac's son chipped me to score. We got back into the dressing room and Alan quipped, 'Pav, some things just never fucking change.' I'm thinking you cheeky twat. But that is just Alan and his wicked sense of humour. Just when you're not expecting it, bang! He gets you were it hurts. Then David Ginola pulls off his shirt and he is ripped. He looked fantastic; like a Greek god. One of the lads shouts, 'So you've never been in the gym, David?' and 'Nice suntan, handsome.' Great banter, like we'd never been away.

I know that at the time when I was at Newcastle, Keegan didn't really rate me as a keeper, but now there are no hard feelings. I was a young man back then. I have matured and looking back I can see things differently. I understand his position but as a player it was difficult to take.

Steve Black was also there. When Keegan was boss he was always keen to extract the most out of players physically and mentally so Blackie was brought in to do that. I worked with him quite closely at times. He wasn't employed by the club full time but he was often brought in to help players to get fit, or even fitter. Blackie was a bit of a character and always telling jokes.

Don Hutchinson was playing for the Reds on the night. I remember playing against him at St James' Park. I can't recall who he was playing for at the time. It may have been West Ham. He came up to me after the game and said 'Pav, thanks for all that you've done for the Geordies. You are a fantastic man and you have been a fantastic servant for the club'. I was shocked. I didn't know anything about him at the time. I thought why is he telling me this? He didn't need to say that, but he did. He must've felt like he needed to tell me this, which was really good of the guy. He is a real Geordie lad. Maybe it was because he never fulfilled his ambition to play for his home-town club.

The game itself was a bit uneven because most of us were unfit whereas the Liverpool lads have about six or seven exhibition games a year, so they were all reasonably fit. We only come together once every five years or so. I noticed the difference when we ran onto the pitch how out of shape we were. But it was a great day and we made a lot of money for the charity.

CHAPTER 17
SLIPPERY SLOPE

I could not remember the last time I'd been as happy, when Harps called to see whether I'd be interested in going back to Newcastle. It was what I had always wanted. To go back, finish my career on a high at the club I loved and make a few bob at the same time. My wife, Pavla, was a bit indifferent when I told her the news, which soured it a bit. Pavla informed me that she wasn't going to move back to Tyneside and intended to stay in Ostrava with our two children. I thought this was a bit strange because we always went everywhere together. The contract was only for three months, initially, however, so I could see her point of view about changing schools again and disrupting the kids' education.

I could see a change in Pavla around that time. There were complaints that she had followed me around all of her life and never got to do anything she wanted to do. My wife made it known several times she always fancied having a go at skiing but never had the chance. I was never allowed to take part in such activities because as a footballer there was always a risk of serious injury. But, around the Christmas time she went skiing in Italy with a friend of my brother, who was a skiing instructor. I'd met this guy once before. He had stopped at my house in Newcastle with my brother, Milan, for a week. I took them to the match; out for dinner all week; showed them around the town and they thoroughly enjoyed it. Yet this guy appreciated my hospitality so much he betrayed my trust. He was a man with the morals of a sewer rat.

He offered to teach my wife and daughter to ski. At the time, I thought great, Pavla has always wanted to learn, so why not. It will make her happy. She went skiing several times with this guy while I was in my last spell at Newcastle. It wasn't a problem because I had the money. I never thought anything about it until my contract ended at St James' Park and came home. It was then I witnessed a radical change in her behaviour. My suspicions were aroused because she was always on her phone, taking it everywhere she went. She also put a lock on it; not that I ever looked at it. She had never done any of those things in the past. It all came to a conclusion when I startled her walking into our bedroom this one time. She quickly hid her phone under the duvet on the bed. I asked what she was doing. She responded with a lame excuse about wanting to know the time. I pointed out the large digital LED clock behind her. She had guilt written all over her face.

I didn't challenge her at first because I wanted to give her the benefit of the doubt. But later on when I was on our home computer, there were pictures of them both together in a pose that is usually reserved for people in a relationship, not a plutonic friendship. I confronted her after this and she confessed she had been seeing the man. I paid a visit to the snake of a skiing instructor. He nearly shit himself when I knocked on his door. He obviously thought I was going to kick the living daylights out of him, but no. I had no hate, venom nor anger in me. I was calmness personified. He denied it but his head was down, his face was coursed with guilt and his body language told me all I needed to know. I warned him to stay away from my family and that he would be sorry if I ever saw him near my kids.

My brother asked why I didn't kick the shit out of the man. I told him if anyone deserved a beating it was my wife. She was the one who encouraged the man. She had, to my knowledge, remained faithful for 21 years. It was like I never knew the woman. The first time someone pays her a bit of attention and she cheats on me. I got propositioned by women on numerous occasions when we were together and never took advantage of it. You get more than your fair share of interest than the average man, being a professional sportsman, yet I resisted that temptation. But not only did she cheat on me, she used our daughter to cover up the web of lies she left behind. I can never forgive her for that.

Friends later tipped me off that she was phoning people saying I was going crazy. But she was trying to manipulate the situation in her favour. I wanted to leave but it was too close to Christmas so I decided to stay for the children. It was the worst Festive period of my life. She wanted to save our marriage and try to fix it but I felt betrayed and couldn't because, in essence, our life together had been a lie. As I said, I wasn't angry, just disappointed.

A couple of months after I found out, about my wife's infidelity, I went out every night with friends for dinner, a few drinks and stopped at my brother's house. It was hardly a *News of the World* drugs and drink binging meltdown. And I never went with another woman in revenge. But it was upsetting all the same. Pavla was always calling to find out where I was and in the end she said it would be better if I left; I agreed. I packed my bags the following day and moved in with my mother, as you do. I was worried about how my mother would react. She was an old woman and I feared she may have a heart attack. But my mother was fine with it and revealed Pavla had mentioned getting divorced when I was back in Newcastle. My mother never told me until that moment.

I was bitter for about three months afterwards. I wasn't working at that time as well so I never had anything to preoccupy myself with. But then I woke up one morning and felt like a new man. I said to myself, right, that's it. Let's get on with the rest of your life. Now, I feel nothing for her. It's like I never knew her and she feels like a stranger. If it wasn't for the fact I need to see my children I wouldn't ever speak to her. That is the toughest part of our split. I never get to see my children as much as I want to. But my ex wife, she is dead to me now.

I know this isn't Richard Burton and Liz Taylor or Elvis and Priscilla Pressley. And I'm not the first one to go through this but the biggest heartache was using one of my children to conspire against me, while manipulating the youngest child. I always joke with my friends to be wary if any of their wives or girlfriends want to go skiing or take their phones to the toilet.

The year I had off was one of the hardest to deal with in my life, not just because of my marriage breakdown. It was the first time I wasn't working. I used to go training every day. So I took up tennis. I got a coach and would go down to the tennis club most mornings. Obviously, I was playing with the club's professional so I was quite competitive. Every time I won a point or rally I would scream in delight, much to the annoyance of the residents living nearby. They would be shouting from their houses: 'zip it boy' or 'shut up', 'it's first thing in the morning' or 'we're trying to sleep'. It was great fun and a perfect outlet to let off steam.

I had an idea to begin a coaching school around this time and set up Pavel's School of Goalkeeping. It was the same period Kevin Keegan had gone back to Newcastle for his second spell in charge. I met with Kevin and pitched the idea to him: I would take goalkeepers from the United academy to train and show them how life was in the Czech Republic and zice-versa; take kids from my home nation and let them see what life was like in the Premier League for a young footballer. I was a bit tentative asking Kevin, because I was never his favourite player, but he was all for it.

I felt the venture had potential. Unfortunately, Keegan left Newcastle and it also coincided with one the biggest economic crashes for the last 20 years. Nevertheless, I set it all up and invited a dozen promising young goalkeepers out to Ostrava where we trained in the mountains. It was a beautiful setting. It cost the kids £750 and the parents who travelled, £500, while the accommodation, meals and flights were all included in the price. The kids also got their training kit and a goody bag all thrown in as well as the coaching sessions each day. However, the parents all thought it was too expensive so in the end the idea didn't really get off the ground after the first trip.

After a year off I got a job coaching the goalkeepers at my old club, Banik. I thought it was too good to be true because they offered me a decent salary for the Czech Republic. The first year was great; they paid my wages into the bank every month. But the same couldn't be said for the second year. Every month when I went to see the chairman about why I hadn't been paid, he would say my salary had to be used to pay off a debt. If it wasn't petrol for the club cars, it was for new training or playing kit or paying the milkman. Then the chairman would say I have plenty money from my career in football so I wasn't a priority. Yet I was still at training every day, employing my skills to coach and using petrol to get to and from work. After eleven months of excuses and without any wages I quit.

I had an opportunity to sue Banik through the Czech FA but refused to go down the line several other people were using. I approached the club and we came to an agreement that they would pay me in instalments. Banik was sold soon after this agreement was put in place. But the new owner and I met up to resolve the matter because, despite his promises, the former chairman did not meet any of these instalments. Instead there were several lines of excuses to why he couldn't pay, which were as pathetic as: a headache, to the dog ate my homework. After another four years, of excuses and procrastination, my debt was finally settled in 2012.

After I quit Banik, in 2010, I had a year coaching the Czech Republic Under-19 team, which was a good experience, before I was offered a role at Sparta Prague in 2011. I am always happier when I am training with the goalkeepers. I've never had any ambitions or interest to be a manager or the first team coach. Although it looked like I was going to be offered the Beira Mar job after Manuel Cajuda was sacked. Thankfully I escaped that frightening episode. Likewise, coaching the goalkeepers has no appeal to Sparta manager Zdeněk Ščasný. He does not interfere with my training and I do not meddle in first team affairs. He lets me get on with it.

I always tell my goalkeepers they must have the right attitude and discipline if they are going to make it. I like to teach them good habits and lifestyle choices. In some ways I'm more than a coach. I'm more like a mentor and father figure to my keepers.

I have a great life in Prague. I coach the first team goalkeepers in the morning and then train the juniors in the afternoon, although I only get paid for coaching the first team squad goalkeepers. I spend between four and five hours a day on the training pitch. I would work from 7am to 7pm or longer. It's one of the best jobs in the world. But coaching at St James' Park, could there ever be a better position than that?

CHAPTER 18
BEST NEWCASTLE TEAM

Shay Given/Steve Harper

Steve Howey Philippe Albert John Beresford

Robert Lee, Barry Venison, Peter Beardsley, David Ginola

Andy Cole, Alan Shearer, Les Ferdinand

It was always going to be difficult to select the finest players I've played with at St James' Park because we had so many great footballers at the club during my time. As you can see from my selection it is based on, an all out attack, we can score more goals than you Kevin Keegan paradigm. I challenge all Newcastle United fans to choose a different or better side.

The goalkeeper position is a challenging one because I believe Steve Harper and Shay Given were both fantastic goalkeepers and great servants to Newcastle United. Kenny Dalglish brought in Shay to replace me in 1997. He, like myself, struggled to win over the United supporters in his first season. It was difficult for him to prevail over Magpies' fans, as well, because I was a fans' favourite at the time. When Dalglish got sacked, new manager, Ruud Gullit wasn't totally convinced by Shay. Admittedly, the Irishman's kicking wasn't great and he never felt comfortable collecting crosses.

When Shay first came in I didn't feel he was a better goalkeeper than me. But he worked hard at his game and went on to become one of the best goalkeepers in the Premier League. He had a fantastic attitude on the training ground. His application and dedication, like Steve's, was exemplary. A great shot stopper, agile and athletic between the posts, Shay is a credit to the Magpies' history.

Steve Harper is one of my closest friends in Newcastle. I saw him blossom, in a Hans Christian Andersen way, from an ugly duckling to a swan. He started as an awkward teenager with me before being sent out on loan a few times. Every time he came back, from these spells, I could see a change in him and he continued to improve.

He was always a calm, confident and assured goalkeeper. Nothing seemed to deter him. He played with no fear, good with both feet and was excellent in a one on one situation. As a goalkeeper you have to stand up for as long as you can in these circumstances. You have to make it difficult for the striker and get him to make a choice. If you go down too soon you make it easier for him. He was always comfortable coming off his line for crosses as well.

Harps stood in Shay's shadow for a long time but, every time he stepped in for the Irishman, he proved what a fantastic goalkeeper he was. It was a long time coming but he finally established himself as the club's number one goalkeeper. Steve was a fantastic servant to Newcastle United.

John Beresford would line up on the left of a back three. Bez had a great left foot; pace and could get up and help the attack and get back and defend as well. Some of the lads used to take this piss out of Bez because they said he squealed like a woman when he got tackled. He was very self deprecating and used to laugh and joke about this. But he always got stuck in and was a tough tackler.

Steve Howey would be to the right of my back three. Steve began life as a striker, before Kevin Keegan converted him to a centre back. I believe if it wasn't for all of his injuries he could've gone on to greater things. He had all the right attributes of a central defender. He could head the ball; comfortable on the ball; quick for a big lad and could read the game very well.

Philippe Albert would complete my back three. The big Belgian brought something to the Premier League many had not seen before in a centre half. He could dribble; had wonderful vision; good in the air; fantastic left foot and could score goals. How many defenders in the world have the flair, composure and audacity to chip Peter Schmeichel, rated as one of the Premier League's greatest goalkeepers? He had the skill of a midfield player, poised, never flustered and always comfortable on the ball. He was another who had some career-threatening injuries but managed to bounce back.

Barry Venison would be at the heart of my midfield. Venners began life with us at right back but was moved to the middle of the park by Keegan and I felt it was his best position. He wasn't the greatest footballer I ever played with but what a man to have on the pitch beside you. He brought players together, screamed, shouted and bollocked them. He wasn't everyone's cup of tea but the rollickings were never personal with Barry. He was always honest with you and I appreciated that. It was always for the greater good of the team. He was a true inspiration to everyone who played with him.

There have been many conspiracy theories to why or how Newcastle contrived to throw away the title in 1996. But if Venners had been in the heart of our engine room, maybe, we would have won the Premier League crown that year. He had the experience of winning a top flight title and playing in big games with Liverpool. He would have held his nerve, kept calm and brought his team mates into line when we were up against it or struggling.

With his application, determination and dedication, Venners would be my captain. How many players do you know who would tell Kevin Keegan he wasn't good enough to play anymore?

Robert Lee would play on the right of midfield, where he first started for us under Keegan. I know he preferred playing in the centre but because I have so many great players at my disposal, the former Charlton man will have to make do with a place on the right.

Bobby, alongside Pedro and Steve Howey, was Kevin Keegan's favourite player. He was a fantastic midfielder in my time at the club. He could defend; get stuck in; attack and score goals. He wasn't the fastest player running off the ball, although he could run with the ball at pace. He had good skills, an excellent shot; got up and down and tucked in when he needed too.

He was a clever man and always shrewd with his money. I think Rob still has his first pay packet. He's tighter than a camel's backside in a sandstorm. Don't take my word for it, ask any of the players who played with Rob at the time. They all took the piss out of his tight-fisted ways.

Peter Beardsley would play in a withdrawn role in the heart of midfield alongside Venners. I have already spoken at length about how great a player he was. The magic, skill and outrageous goals speak for themselves. I hope Pedro can laugh at this now but I remember he was furious after we all conspired to give him the yellow jersey in training for being the worst player. It was funny because he was such a mild mannered guy who was rarely unruffled by anything. It was so out of character. Yet he blew his top with all of us.

I have nothing but good things to say about Pedro. He used to take my breath away with what he did on the pitch. He did the unexpected all of the time and it was so fast; blink and you missed it. It was generally in the back of the net. He was instinctive and yet he also had a gift in committing defenders and goalkeepers into doing what he wanted them to do. It is little wonder he was called a magician.

It was a pleasure to share the same pitch with Peter Beardsley and other players in my time at the club. In training, I always used to try and stop the likes of Pedro, Alan Shearer, Andy Cole, David Ginola and Les Ferdinand. I thought, if I can stop these guys from scoring then I could cope with anything because there was no one else in the Premier League as good as these players.

There are so many brilliant goals Pedro scored that it is extremely difficult to choose one. But I think I have two goals, which are my favourites; away at Tottenham, in 1993, and a home game against Aston Villa in 1995. At Spurs when he went on a mazy run in the last minute of the clash, beating about four players, before sliding home. Against Villa, it looked as if the ball was glued to his foot as he danced through the Villa defence. I though Paul McGrath's head was going to twist off. Lionel Messi or Cristiano Ronaldo would be proud to have scored goals as good as Beardsley and have their names associated with them. Pedro was scoring goals like that 20 and 30 years ago. I think if Peter Beardsley was playing these days we wouldn't be just talking about Messi and Ronaldo. We would be waxing lyrical over Beardsley.

David Ginola would play on the left of my midfield. I had never seen anyone quite like Ginola. I know it is a bit of cliché, that he was incredible for the first six months, but he was. Maybe we say that because we'd become accustomed and too familiar with his unusual Gallic flair, I don't know. Like Pedro, David, was another who would have you on the edge of your seat. I had the best view in the house, almost, from where I was standing. He had flair, two great feet and he had this remarkable trick. The one where he had two players on him with his back to goal: he'd drop his left shoulder to feint left and then turn 180 degrees to the right and leave defenders catching flies. It was the same trick every time. Defenders knew it but they couldn't stop him.

I remember when we played Middlesbrough at home at the beginning of the 1995-96 season. In dressing room after the game, David chuckled, 'I thought I broke his back! I heard it snap when I turned him.' He was talking about Boro defender Neil Cox, who was a good defender, but Ginola made him look very ordinary.

He was never a player who would track back and defend. There were times when we felt we were playing with ten men against 11. That was after the first six months, maybe, and then the better teams got wise to us and could punish us. Kevin did try and get the Frenchman to tuck back in but it was tough for him because he'd never done it before. Why didn't he track back? Unlike other pass and move flair players, Ginola, was a dribbler and, he used an enormous amount of effort and energy taking on players, arguably more than anyone else. It takes longer to recover from such exertion. Saying that, what a footballer.

Andy Cole would form part of a three pronged attack in my line up. Andy was like a breath of fresh air when he first arrived at St James' Park. He was as quick as anyone I have ever seen. And he was perfect foil for Pedro. Beardsley would instinctively know where he was or could find him and Coley was on to it in a flash. He had an amazing strike rate, which would have been all the more better if he didn't have that mini drought before he left. We were all sorry to see him go but he went on to have a fantastic career at Manchester United when he left Tyneside.

Alan Shearer, obviously, is the greatest goalscorer in the Premier League so it goes without saying, he would spearhead the attack. Shearer is another player where you think, what can I add or say about him that hasn't been already said. I used to go home black and blue after training because he hit the ball so hard in shooting practice. I'm sure Shay Given, Steve Harper and Shaka Hislop did as well. It was a shock the first time because no one had hit the ball at me with such intensity before. Then when he'd put the ball past you he would say something, taking the piss, and it would drive you on to do better.

People back in the Czech Republic would ask about Alan all of the time. I used to tell them, I don't know where he got his power and strength because I never saw him in the gym. Yet when you hit him in training or a game, it would be like you'd hit a tree. And that would be everyone, not just the smaller players with a slight build, everyone. I'm 6ft 2in and I used to bounce off him. He wasn't one of the tallest players but was there any players better heading the ball? His timing and anticipation was perfect. In all great players, they haven't learned it, they are born with it. Alan made everything look simple and it wasn't. Scoring goals is one of the hardest skills in football. That is why so many millions of pounds are spent every season on strikers. And of course, Shearer also leads the attack for having the most exciting goal celebration ever witnessed; yes, I'm taking the piss, Alan.

Les Ferdinand would play alongside Shearer up front in my side. Les was a great signing for the club. I remember people questioning the £6m fee at the time because he was 29 and there would be no sell on; although the club got that money back after two years. There were also questions about his fitness. Anyone who saw him stripped, training or on a Saturday, would tell you, he was as fit as they come. He had an incredible leap to head the ball, quick and had a nice habit of scoring goals.

Critics and pundits all said Shearer and Ferdinand couldn't work together because they were too similar. They were both target men, yet they gelled perfectly. If you go through all of the goals Alan scored in his time at Newcastle you'll find that only Laurent Robert and Nobby Solano made more goals for him than Les. How many seasons did Les and Alan spend together? One! That is a staggering fact. Imagine how many goals they would've netted between them had Kenny Dalglish not sold Les? It doesn't bear thinking about. If you do, it'll probably drive you to drinking.

CHAPTER 19
BEST INTERNATIONAL TEAM

Petr Kouba

Radoslav Latal, Antolin Alcaraz, Filippo Galli, Marek Jankulovski

Pavel Nedved, Andrea Pirlo, Pep Guardiola, Patrik Berger

Jan Koller, Roberto Baggio

Once again I was privileged to have played with so many great players in my career. Having the choice of picking two teams has been a bit of a blessing, although it hasn't made it any easier. I had the pleasure of playing for the Czech Republic when we were ranked in the top three for most of my international playing days, so it will come as no surprise that several of my home nation colleagues feature heavily in the side. I was also lucky enough to play alongside some of the greatest players in world football following my spell in Italy, while there is a surprise package from when I plied my trade in Portugal.

Petr Kouba is an easy choice to make as my number one. My Czech international team mate wasn't the best player in training but he was the most talented goalkeeper I played with. He took up life as a goalkeeper quite late at 15-years-old. Prior to that gymnastics was his chosen vocation and you could see that when he played. He was quick, agile and had fantastic reflexes. He could almost spring across the goal line.

Kouba's father, Pavel, was also an exceptional Czech international goalkeeper. He was between the posts when Czechoslovakia lost 3-1 to Brazil in the 1962 World Cup. It's unusual to have a father and son combination play for the national teams in the final of a major tournament.

Kouba wasn't the tallest but he was the best all round goalkeeper I ever trained with or saw play.

Radoslav Latal would be my choice at right back, although he was equally comfortable playing further up the field, such was his versatility. Latal started his career in Sigma Olomouc, in the Czech league, but I came across him on international duty. Latal later went on to play for Schalke 04 in Germany, where he won the UEFA Cup in 1997. He was fast, strong and could score goals, which was a bonus for a defender. He was always totally committed and gave his all to the cause.

Antolin Alcaraz would be the surprise choice in my international team because he is relatively unknown. I met him as a young, promising centre half at Beira Mar. He was tall, good in the air, strong and fast. He wasn't great in a positional sense as a youngster but most centre halves don't come into their own until they are in their mid twenties.

Alcaraz later got a move to Wigan Athletic before transferring to Everton with his former boss Roberto Martinez. He then became an international for Paraguay. The youngster was one of the key players in our promotion from the second tier to the first in my second season in Portugal.

Filippo Galli would provide the calming influence and experience alongside Alcaraz. Galli was a fantastic professional and a great example to everyone on and off the field. He was another who gave 100 per cent to the cause and never gave up. This is one of the first attributes I would look for in a player. He had an amazing career at AC Milan with the likes of Ruud Gullit, Marco van Basten and Frank Rijkaard when they won the European Cup in the 1990s. He was always composed on the ball, versatile and brave and had great technique. I think he was about 36 when he played for Brescia but could still mix it and read almost any situation.

Marek Jankulovski is another former international playing colleague of mine. Like Latal, he was as comfortable further forward in an attacking role as he was as a defender. I met Jankulovski prior to the Euro 2000 championships when he was called into the squad from the under-21 side. I knew about him, however, because he is from Ostrava and played for my old club Banik. Ironically, I met him in the airport soon after the Euro 2000 championships. I was coming back from Napoli while he was on his way to Napoli. He eventually signed for the Italian outfit. He also went on to play for AC Milan, where he won a Champions League title after they beat Liverpool.

He had a fantastic left foot; versatile; great technique and could play anywhere down the left side. He could score goals, had pace and was also a great crosser of the ball.

Pavel Nedved is arguably one of the best footballers of his generation. Nedved was probably the best Czech Republic footballer I ever played with and is possibly the most decorated player in our history. The midfielder helped Juventus to the European Champions League final, won the UEFA Cup, Cup Winners Cup; Serie A titles and the Ballon d'Or, as well as several other individual awards.

The Italians nicknamed him Furia Ceca, which translates, blind fury. Nedved was a complete player. He had everything in his armoury. He had two good feet, could defend, attack, pass, score goals and his work rate was phenomenal. He never stopped running for 90 minutes.

Pep Guardiola is probably better known for being a manager at Barcelona and Bayern Munich than being a top footballer. Pep was the pivot or foundation Johan Cruff built his 'Dream Team' in the early 1990s. The club lifted their first European Cup, in 1992, with Guardiola central to Barca's success. The club have always had several more glamorous superstars playing in their side. Yet, he remained at the heart of their midfield for the next 11 years, quietly and diligently going about his business while the others claimed the spotlight. You have to be someone special to play for the Catalan giants for that length of time.

I met Pep in Brescia, of course. He was always employed as a defensive midfielder throughout his career. Unlike the traditional defensive midfield players in British football, he wasn't a hard man, like David Batty or Roy Keane, who were tearing into tackles. He always seemed to be one step ahead of other players, reading moves before they happened. It was a great gift. You cannot teach players this. You are either born with it or you're not born with it. Guardiola was always composed on the ball; had great vision and was an excellent passer of the ball.

Andrea Pirlo is another player I met while playing for Brescia. He was just starting out as a youngster at that time and wasn't the rounded player we see today. He is a Bresciano, which means he is a native of Brescia. Pirlo started his career with the club but then moved on to Italian giants Inter Milan, who loaned him back to us. AC Milan then signed him and before he moved on to Juventus.

He had the honour of becoming Brescia's youngest ever debutant, when making his first appearance for the Lombardy based club. You could see he had the potential to be a great player and go on and have a celebrated career. It was no coincidence he was part of the team that finished seventh in Serie A, the club's best ever finish. He obviously went on to bigger and better things, winning World Cup; Champions League and Serie A titles, but he was instrumental for us that season. He has also earned over 100 caps for Italy.

Like Guardiola, Pirlo is another defensive, deep lying but creative midfielder. He was a set piece expert; majestic passer of the ball and remarkable vision to pick out a player.

Patrick Berger was another player I had the privilege to play with. Patrick had fantastic ability. He was very tall, but despite that, had a great touch. He could play anywhere down the left or through the middle. Another great left footed player, who always broke with pace and had an eye for a goal. It was a pity he was troubled by injuries throughout his career. Despite that he still managed to win several honours in club football. Berger was part of Liverpool's treble winning side of 2001, when the Reds won the FA Cup, UEFA Cup and League Cup. He had a powerful shot and almost hit it the ball as hard as Shearer. Arguably the best left footed player I came across in football.

Jan Koller was possibly one of the finest target men in the world on his day. I was introduced to big Jan when he joined the international squad for the first time and we shared a room. He used to call me Mr Srnicek because that was how people formally addressed others when they didn't know them. But we became good friends when Koller informed me he was in the army with my brother, Milan. He was a lovely man.

Sparta Prague supporters were sceptical when he first signed for the club because he was an ungainly striker with big feet and not very agile. He took long strides and ran like a horse and everyone used to take the piss out of him. But then his career kicked off when he moved to Lokeren in Belgium. Koller got transferred to Anderlecht, then Borussia Dortmund winning titles and accolades on the way. He started as a goalkeeper, originally, and once replaced Jens Lehmann in a Dortmund game after the former Arsenal man was sent off.

He had a distinguished international career, scoring 55 goals in 91 outings for the national team. No one has scored more goals for the Czech Republic. He was a beast of a striker and no defender enjoyed playing against him. Koller was also great defending corners and was often heading balls away from defensive situations. Not the most technically gifted striker but a right handful. He wasn't quick over ten yards but once he got started he was so powerful you couldn't catch him. He could hold it up well and because his build was awkward, and big, no one could get the ball off him. He rarely put his foot through the ball, when striking it, Jan nearly always used the side of his foot. But he generated an enormous amount of power from those gigantic size 14 boots! His feet were so big that Puma, our sponsors in Euro 2000, didn't have any boots big enough for him, so they had to make some specially.

Roberto Baggio would be in everyone's world XI. What can I add to what I have already said about one of the best footballers who ever played? He lit the blue touch paper in the 1990 World Cup, in Italy, and continued to illuminate every football pitch he ever played on. Baggio wasn't called the Divine Ponytail for no reason. I think everyone who has played with Roberto will have felt blessed. I was lucky enough to play with him for two seasons at Brescia. Admittedly, he was coming to the end of his playing career but you could still see he was a marvellous player.

He was deadly around the opposition's box and 30 yards from goal. Probably the most technically gifted player I have had the good fortune to play with. Obviously, the legs weren't as quick as they were in his autumn years but his vision, brain and reading of a situation was fatal for the opposition. It was a pleasure and privilege to not only play with the footballer but to get to know him as well. He was a lovely man.

CHAPTER 20
THE NAKED CHEF

I have always dreamt of owning a small restaurant when I retire from football. Maybe I'd call it Pav's Place. You will laugh when I tell you the idea sprung to mind while I was living in Newcastle. I know, hardly the cuisine capital of the world, but then again, neither was the Czech Republic for that matter. The food in my home country is quite bland in comparison to those nations where gastronomy is a speciality. Like other countries, we had our traditional fare, such as: roast pork, dumplings and sauerkraut. But I'm not sure how it would stand up against others on the *Great British Bake Off*, *Masterchef* or *Fanny's Kitchen*.

I wouldn't employ a chef and neither would there be any waiters. I would like to do it all myself: cooking, waiting on the tables and serving drinks. That is why I would like a small place with only five choices: five starter courses; five main courses and five desserts. I would do same with the wine list, only five bottles of red wine, five white wine and five different beers. Maybe in time I would increase it to ten of each. But if I did that the intimacy would be lost on what I was trying to create. And that is to engage in conversation and enjoy the food, drink and ambience. The Italians are masters at this.

I told my friends and colleagues, past and present, in the Czech Republic about what I ate when I first played for Newcastle United and they wouldn't believe me. The attention to detail is so meticulous these days, where a player's diet is concerned. They would laugh if I told them how we all salivated at the prospect of calling into the Wetherby Whaler, in North Yorkshire, when coming home from an away match. It is arguably the finest fish and chip shop in the country.

It was the first time I had experienced a chip butty. I looked at the bread roll, with butter slapped on it and I was a bit sceptical at first. I'd never witnessed anything like it in my life! It looked revolting. But I watched the lads tuck in so I thought what the hell and, followed suit, placing chips between the buttered roll. It tasted fantastic. I wasn't so keen on the batter around the fish, so I used to peel it off. But I loved the chip butties. I used to smother mine with ketchup at first. The lads would be shouting, 'Pav, brown sauce is the best, try that.' I was gradually persuaded to use brown sauce before graduating on to curry sauce with my chip butties. Hardly Beluga Caviar or Haute Cuisine, I know, but man it was tasty.

I used to go home to the Czech Republic and tell people how we had fish with batter on, chips, or chicken in bread crumbs with chips, after a game. They would say, 'you're crazy!' And the cans of coke we would drink. As many and as much as we could drink or wanted. We could've eaten grass; it wouldn't have mattered, as long as we produced the goods on the pitch. My first visit to the Wetherby Whaler wasn't under Kevin Keegan or Kenny Dalglish. I first went to the Whaler under Ossie Ardiles, but it has always been a tradition with all footballers and not just United players. Football teams from all over the country still frequent the chip shop. I should get free fish and chips for life now, after that plug.

I also remember my first bacon sarnie. It was delicious. It wasn't long before an English cooked breakfast was a regular feature on the Srnicek kitchen table. I used to go to Harry Ramsden's fish and chip shop at the Metro Centre as well. I remember this one time asking for the biggest fish they had. It was the haddock. After I devoured the lot a waitress came over with a sheet of paper and asked me to sign it. I thought she was asking for an autograph at first. But no, I was signing a special certificate because she said, 'Not many people can finish the large haddock dish.' I was embarrassed. I was thinking I bet she thinks I'm a right greedy bastard.

I had my first, what you would call, Sunday roast, when my wife and I were invited around to one of the players' houses. I think it was either Kevin Scott or Benny Kristensen who introduced me to the traditional roast beef Sunday lunch. It looked different to what we had eaten before but the Yorkshire puddings and gravy was nice. I loved the conventional British breakfasts, dinner and fish and chips. Everything was new to my wife and I. I had my first taste of Chinese, Italian and Indian food when I moved to Newcastle. Remember I lived under the old Communist regime and our food was plain, although I did, and still do, enjoy it.

One of the first dinner parties I was invited too in Newcastle had a buffet laid on. On the table, among other things, there was a selection of small sandwiches and crisps. I loved the texture and combination when I ate them. So every now and then, when I visit Geordieland, I'll buy a sandwich and a packet of salt and vinegar crisps. I'll go and sit in a park somewhere; watch the world go by and eat them. In the Czech

Republic I generally eat Italian food but when I'm visiting friends in Newcastle I'll eat Chinese or Indian. The Chinese and Indian restaurants in my home country aren't as good as those in Geordieland.

My diet radically changed when I went to play in Italy at Brescia. There wasn't really a special diet when I played football in England. You could go up to the buffet table as many times as you wanted for lunch before and after a match or following training. Players would pile it on: fish, chicken, beef and pork, all on the one plate. You generally couldn't see who was carrying the food because it was piled so high. We would shout, 'Who's behind the plate' or 'Do you eat that or just climb it'? Great fun but I'm not so sure it was so good for your digestive system. I couldn't wait for every meal time when I was at Brescia because the food in Italy was first-class. In training I was almost salivating at the prospect of having lunch. There was never any rush. We would take our time, get some rest and then we would be back out for an afternoon session. After that work out we would be back at the dining table eating and taking our time over several more courses. This is the Italian way. Breakfast, lunch and dinner are big occasions in Italy and I really enjoyed this cultural aspect of the Italian lifestyle. Now, at home, I love cooking Italian dishes and having the odd glass of red wine. The perfect combination for me would be the Italian lifestyle married with English football.

I was very fortunate when I went to live in Italy. Brescia isn't the nicest town to live but I moved to Lake Garda, which was about 50 miles away. I had a house, garden with a swimming pool, overlooking the lake; something I never had in England. I'd sit on the terrace in my garden every day and eat Italian food. I love Parma ham with melon. My neighbour used to say to me, 'Pav, you don't need anything else when the weather is as good as this.' He was right. You didn't need any more than this. The melon gives you the vitamins and the ham gives you strength. I used to walk into the town and there was a fruit and vegetable stall. An old woman used to serve me a mixed salad in a brown paper bag. I had this lifestyle for four years and I loved it. I still have the house but I rent it out because I live and work in Prague.

I was a frequent visitor to the New Rendezvous in Darras Hall after I met Kevin Lau, who owned the restaurant, when I dropped off my daughter, Vendy, at school. And when I'm back in Newcastle I'm a frequent visitor to Laus 202 on Newgate Street. It's all a bit different from when I used to shop in Tesco at Kingston Park. At first my wife and I used to look at the pictures on tins because we couldn't translate the language. This was all part of the learning process and excitement of starting a new life in a foreign country.

One of the highlights of my time living in Sheffield was learning to cook Chinese. I remember visiting a Chinese supermarket in the Steel City and asking the store manager whether he could find someone who could teach me. I was willing to pay for the lessons. Eventually I met this Chinese guy and he wouldn't take any money off me. I went around to his house and watched how he prepared the food. After this he told me to go and buy all of the ingredients and he came around to my house and I cooked for him. He must have been a good teacher because he said my dishes were perfect.

Food isn't my only favourite cultural pastime because I also love music. I would never claim to be an expert like David Ginola, but I love to listen to music to help me unwind. I have quite an eclectic taste in music from Czech folk, pop and classic rock. Not many people will know this but I'm partial to a bit of a Karaoke sing song. What song do I sing? Nothing by a British or American artist or band, although I do like, Bruce Springsteen, Phil Collins, Queen, U2, Chris Rea and some American country music. I went to see Chris Rea in concert in Prague and, despite being a fan of his music, he was disappointing. There wasn't much interaction with the audience and I got the feeling he didn't want to be there. I also saw the Lighthouse Family. I don't feel comfortable singing in English because it's not my first language so I only sing songs from Czech artists. I remember Budgie was always up exercising his tonsils, if he got the chance, when we went out. My old friend and colleague loved to get up and sing. In fact Kevin Keegan was a good singer too. I started to play the guitar about three years ago. I got it as a Christmas present from my son Maxim. But since I came to Sparta Prague as a coach I haven't had time to learn properly. It is another one for the future bucket list that I need to master.

My first music purchase was an Erasure CD when I moved to Newcastle. I also remember buying a Queen CD the day Freddie Mercury died, although I wasn't to know that at the time of paying for it. The shock of me buying it probably killed him. My favourite Queen song is *Too Much Love Will Kill You*. That line 'I'm just a shadow of the man I used to be,' is the story of my life, when I look back. No, put those violins away guys. My favourite U2 song is *Sometimes You Can't Make It Up On Your Own*.

Obviously I couldn't afford to buy any records or CDs when I lived at home. We only had the radio to listen too. I can't name one Czech artist I liked because there were so many. Maybe Karel Gott, he was dubbed the Czech Frank Sinatra. There was no western influence on our ears from outside the Czech Republic. We only got local singers, for local people on the radio. Not quite like the *League of Gentlemen* in Royston Vasey, but you'll get the idea.

When I moved to Newcastle I used to watch *Top of the Pops*, listen to the radio and bought a top of the range CD music centre, with massive speakers. I watched a lot of Czech DVDs, and when we got satellite TV I could watch all the shows from home. My wife and I used to watch *Coronation Street*. But on the way to games the lads used to bring all sorts of videos. Pedro introduced me to *Only Fools and Horses*, which was funny. The lads also brought videos of *Auf Wiedersehen, Pet*, another series I enjoyed. Of course there was the infamous Tino moment when he asked Keegan to play his porn video. Kevin nearly shit himself and immediately jumped up to turn it off. Tino was saying, 'No, no, no gaffer, eets my meesis.' We were all doubled up on the team bus.

I used to watch the football on Sky and *Match of the Day*. But Match of the day was frustrating when Alan Hansen was on. He made me angry most of the time; always slagging people off and he made a living out of it. You just wonder whether Simon Cowell was influenced by the Scot. I didn't mind Gary Linekar. Sky football was excellent. The way they developed the programme over the years was great. I was a fan of Chris Evans when he did *TFI Friday* and *Don't Forget your Toothbrush*. But like I've said several times in the book already, there was something extraordinary about this era or time, culturally. Music, television and sport were evolving into something special. I got the feeling there was a definitive spirit of an age. It is always hard to define or explain while you're living through it or even looking back on it. I know I don't get the same emotion about the here and now but maybe that is because I was a young man looking forward back then. Nevertheless, it was a great time to live and play football for Newcastle and the Czech Republic.

CHAPTER 21
EPILOGUE

I've always kept an eye on my old club since I left St James' Park and it's saddened me it hasn't built on the dreams of what Kevin Keegan and Sir John Hall envisioned in the early 1990s. Kenny Daglish came in and ultimately punctured the wheels of progress, while Ruud Gullit's biggest faux pas was underestimating the size of the club. Sir Bobby Robson was then appointed and revitalised the Magpies before Graeme Souness did another spectacular piece of work dismantling Robson's rejuvenation restoring United's fortunes, not only in the Premier League but on the European stage. Glenn Roeder had the best intentions but didn't get the time to complete the job. The same could be said for Chris Hughton, while Joe Kinnear was an astonishing appointment for all the wrong reasons.

My home town team is Banik Ostrava yet I work for Sparta Prague. The Banik supporters can't get their head around this. First and foremost I am a professional and, second, I'm not going to refuse to work for the biggest club in the Czech Republic. Yet if I left Sparta, for whatever reason, and another club came in for me, I would give the same 100 per cent commitment and dedication to the cause. In Sparta, my salary is three times what it was in Banik, yet I still give the same loyalty and dedication at both clubs. Newcastle is, and always will be, a fans club. And I always got the feeling Daglish, Gullit, Souness and Sam Allardyce were only there for the money. They never felt anything for the club, had any passion for the Geordies or bought into what it is like living in the North-East.

I could be at one end of the world and if I got a call to go back to Newcastle, I would crawl over broken glass to be a part of something special again. This doesn't just apply to me; there are several other former players, coaches and managers who would do the same. Even if I was a coach at Barcelona, Real Madrid or Bayern Munich, I would pack my case and get the first available horse and cart back to Tyneside.

Newcastle need another Kevin Keegan, Bobby Robson or someone with a connection or feeling for the club, city and North-East and turn around its fortunes. I would love to have played for Sir Bobby. I have only heard good things about him. I met him once and he said, 'It is a privilege to meet a true Newcastle legend.' It was lovely of him to say something like that. You need to get players playing for you like Sir Bobby did. I can't say anyone really wanted to play for Daglish, Souness or Allardyce. It doesn't have to be a Geordie. Someone like Jurgen Klopp would have been a good choice because he gives 100 per cent wherever he goes. I don't mean to be disrespectful to Steve McClaren but Newcastle missed out there and United's loss will be Liverpool's gain. The same can be said about Pep Guardiola. He managed Barcelona with all the will and passion in the world. Then he moved to Bayern Munich and gave the same enthusiasm and commitment to the cause of the German giants. Can you say that about Daglish, Souness and Allardyce?

I thought, fantastic, when Ruud Gullit was named Newcastle manager. I never knew him personally. He was one of the greatest footballers of his generation and had managerial success at Chelsea. But as everyone knows the greatest players don't necessarily make the greatest managers. You look at the Premier League and the most successful managers since its inauguration have been Sir Alex Ferguson, Arsene Wenger and Jose Mourinho. None of those could be classed as being greats in their playing days. Yet, in contrast to that, Guardiola is proving that a great player can become a great manager. So when Gullit arrived at St James' Park with all the pomp and ceremony of his 'sexy football' paradigm, I'm thinking, yes, Louis van Gaal, Johan Cruff and Guus Hiddink were all good coaches from the Netherlands. I thought Gullit would be the same as them. But then I just don't think he understood the fans, the club or how big it was. And saying the Milan derby was bigger than the Newcastle v Sunderland derby just showed how out of touch he was.

The clashes with Alan Shearer, Rob Lee and Shay Given didn't help. Putting Alan Shearer on the bench for a Tyne and Wear derby has to be one of the biggest calamities a manager has ever made. I'm not saying you can't put Shearer on the bench, but Alan is no ordinary player. He's Alan Shearer. Sir Alex Ferguson has put big stars on the bench but he has done it with style and class. Another mistake Gullit made was that he thought he was bigger than the club, and no one is bigger than the club, not even Alan Shearer.

I had high hopes when Keegan went back to Newcastle. But it was inevitable Kevin would walk away. He is a man who likes to be in total control. He has someone above him buying and selling players and he was left to just manage what was brought in. He knew the blueprint for success and it wasn't the one Mike Ashley had of buying young potential and selling it on once it matured. Keegan liked to nurture talent and build success on the back of it.

I'm not a believer in the European concept where a manager is given a group of players selected by a scout or scouting team and he just manages or coaches them. The manager must have the power to pick his own players and manage the team accordingly. Have Newcastle had any success with the model since Mike Ashley took over? No, he hasn't accomplished anything aside from qualifying for the Europa League, once, in his eight years at the helm.

Sir John Hall never interfered with team affairs in the five years Keegan was in charge. Kevin asked for a player and Sir John would get the player for him. Yet in Europe this is common place. All chairmen, directors and owners interfere with team affairs and want their favourite players in the starting line up. I don't know Mike Ashley. Everything I hear about him reveals he is a great businessman. And when you look at his record in the business industry it is exemplary. But in football he will always be remembered for sacking Kevin Keegan and Alan Shearer; two of the biggest icons, heroes and legends in the long history of Newcastle United. I don't need to tell anyone the decisions he has made in football don't make sense. As Shearer said 'you can't second guess what he's going to do next' because there is no logic in the choices he makes in football. Even when I think back to the structure he put in place with Denis Wise, Tony Jiminez, Paul Helmsley and Jeff Vetere. It was mind boggling.

Even now he has a chief scout who buys or selects which player is going to join Newcastle. Ashley has had this model in place for over seven years now. Has it been a success? You only need to look at United's league positions since it was put in place to answer that question. One relegation; two close relegation scrapes and, aside from one top five finish, mediocrity and misery in both league and cup competitions. It is an archetype widely popular in Europe and where else does it work, other than the giants of Italy and Spain? It does not work. It is a flawed system.

I would say to Mike Ashley, 'Mike, you've tried this system and it clearly does not work. Give the manager total control over football matters and you concentrate on the commercial side generating revenue for when the boss wants to invest in the team. Why the obsession with buying young players cheap and selling them on? We have to do that at Sparta Prague to survive every season. Newcastle doesn't need to do that. They are a massive club. It does not make any sense. Ashley only needs to look back at how Sir John Hall and Kevin Keegan ran the club.

Sir John would come to the dressing room, wish us luck and shake our hands before every game but never got involved with team affairs. In Europe it is common for owners, chairman and directors to interfere and put pressure on managers to play their favourite players. There once was a time when the Brescia chairman sat on the bench. Could you imagine Roman Abramovich, Daniel Levy or David Sullivan doing that in the Premier League? Moreover, could you imagine if Freddy Shepherd's mother got a say in the team? I was her favourite player, so I would be in every week. Maybe it isn't a bad idea after all.

At Sparta our chairman is an intelligent man and very knowledgeable about the game. But there are other people on the outside who try to exert their influence. I reckon this is one of the problems Ashley has had to face in his time at St James' Park. The United owner isn't a football man and because of this he has been influenced by any Tom, Dick or Harry who once got an orange Trophy football for Christmas as a kid and used jumpers for goalposts.

To have a successful football team on the pitch you have to have everything running smoothly off the pitch. People may say 'Pav, your team wasn't successful' and they'd be right in terms of winning something. But we went very close. After we got promoted we finished 3rd, 6th, 2nd and 2nd and qualified for the Champions League, under Keegan. With a bit more good fortune we could've won something. And when you look back to my time on Tyneside, has anyone ever been as close as us to winning the league? Has Ashley actually learned anything from the club's relegation in 2009?

I know I have said the club should find another Kevin Keegan or Bobby Robson; someone with a connection or feeling for the club. There is another alternative. Why not give the job to a young, promising and hungry coach? If Mike Ashley was to ask me, who I think should get the Newcastle job, I would say why not 'install Václav Jílek as manager?' I have been watching him for the last three years as the Sparta Prague assistant manager and coach. I don't think it was any surprise that we won the treble in 2014 because he was pulling the strings behind the manager. It was the first time Sparta had won the title in four years. He was never the best footballer. He played in the third and fourth tier of the Czech Republic leagues. But his knowledge of the game is phenomenal.

Jílek combined his lower status as a footballer by teaching maths and physical education in a Czech school. But these days he has taken it upon himself to become a student of football. He studies, watches and learns from all of the great coaches and managers of the past and the here and now. He has even started to learn English, so he can read all the British coaching manuals.

It was tough when he first started out coaching because he didn't have the respect of the first team players. They used to look down on him because he didn't have an illustrious career. Sparta players felt as if they were superior to him because they were playing for the biggest club in the Czech Republic. Yet he eventually earned the respect of the footballers after

Jilek's methods began to bear fruit. The Sparta coach's stock has risen so much that the Czech Republic FA now consults with him over most of the nation's footballing matters. That is the reverence and esteem he now holds in my home nation.

I have no doubt Jilek has the presence and personality to be a success in the Premier League, Serie A, La Liga or Bundesliga. And there is no doubt he could handle big name players or superstars. His training methods are interesting, fresh and he introduces different exercises every session. He's never satisfied. He's always looking at other peoples' methods, such as Guardiola and Mourinho, trying to improve on their techniques as well as his own. He's obsessed with the game.

I am convinced Jilek, if he is given the chance, will be as successful as a Jose Mourinho or Arsene Wenger, if he is given between three and five years at a club. One or two years do not give you enough time to assemble a squad and get them playing the way you want them too. Slovakian outfit MSK Zilina appointed a relatively unknown manager, Adrian Gul'a, in 2013, with a five year plan, after his success with second tier outfit Trencin. In his three years with the Slovak minnows, the club finished runners up twice before winning the title. Gul'a then joined Zilina and, after a couple of seasons of mediocrity, finishing 7th and 9th, he led them to runners up last term. Why don't Newcastle and other clubs follow that example?

People reading this would say, 'but Pav, Mike Ashley gave Alan Pardew a ten year contract. Surely that is a sign of stability and a plan'. I would say, yes, you would think it was a blueprint for success, yet, Pardew walked away after five years to manage Crystal Palace. He did so because of all the interference and constraints he was put under. You couldn't blame him for doing that. No disrespect to Alan, he is a good coach. He just isn't the right fit for Newcastle. And it's not because he is from London. He's perfect at Palace or West Ham. Why is he not the right fit? He didn't connect with the club, it's fanatical following or the city. Newcastle supporters may look back at his time and say 'he did a good job under difficult circumstances'. However, he hardly endeared himself to the Geordies by his perpetual patronising. They know when someone is being condescending or if someone is falsely taking a moral high ground. Newcastle United supporters know their football. Football is in their blood. It courses through their veins. It has been passed down from generation to generation since the club was formed.

I'm sick of hearing how much money Newcastle United has in the bank. Tired of being told how financially stable the Magpies are compared to the rest of the Premier League. What is the point of having all of that money in the bank when the team is sterile, boring and listless and the club has little ambition? If Mike Ashley doesn't want to spend much money or wants to compromise and get the best value for money, why doesn't he appoint the likes of a Jilek?

If you bring in a Hollywood manager such as Louis van Gaal, he would expect £100m bank roll. But a young hungry manager such as Jilek would be more eager to find or sign similar players to himself: passionate, enthusiastic and dedicated to being successful. He could work on a lower budget and build on it. Ashley could reward his manager with a transfer war chest depending on the club's success or league position? Maybe say to his new manager, 'here's £30m for new players. If you finish in the top ten I'll give you £40m. If you manage to get the club into the Europa League I'll hand over £50m' and so on? That way there is a bonus or incentive to do well.

Another point: what is the obsession with signing French players? Why isn't the scouting network opened up to the rest of the world? Why don't they see how other clubs in Europe can compete with the likes of Barcelona and Real Madrid on a smaller budget? I remember people taking the piss on the Internet about how if you're French, your next club will be Newcastle. Maybe I should be the manager in that case because I have a French passport. But seriously, take FC Porto in Portugal. They have one of the best scouting networks in the world. They buy and sell players yet still remain their nation's most successful club and still compete and triumph in Europe. Only four years ago they won the Europa League.

I've lost my connections with club since Mike Ashley took over which saddens me. Had Freddy Shepherd still been chairman I would be telling them about our young full back, Pavel Kaderabek, who looks likely to move to a German club for between three and four million Euros, a snip for a club like

Newcastle. But Pavel isn't the first precocious young talent I've seen over the last few years. Why don't the club look for players in my home country?
How many other clubs in the Premier League would have 50,000 plus fans turning up every week with little or no hope of winning a title or a cup? Maybe Liverpool or Manchester City supporters would stick with them. But pulling in a crowd of 50,000 for a game in the Championship, as Newcastle did, I'm not so sure. Toon supporters have been fed on a diet of scraps for years now. Imagine if the club won a trophy? They wouldn't go home. They would party for a week, month or even a year. For Newcastle fans the odds of scooping a trophy are like winning the lottery, yet they still live in hope.

Since my association with Newcastle in 1991, the club, directors, owner or chairmen have made some spectacular gaffs when appointing managers. You could probably say, since Joe Harvey was sacked in 1975, the club have only managed to get the right man twice in those 40 years: Kevin Keegan and Sir Bobby Robson. Those don't look great odds, do they? I think many of the club's problems, certainly in the last few years, belongs to nepotism. Appointments have been made because they have been a friend of the owner or chairman.

I have one of the best, if not the best, young goalkeeping coaches in the Czech Republic with me at Sparta in Daniel Zitka. He is, now, one of my best friends in football. I didn't really know him until I arrived at Sparta. But more importantly, I wouldn't employ him because he's my friend. I would employ him because he is one of the best at what he does. At every team I have played at, or coached with, I have always wanted to play with the best players, play for best manager or have the best coach with me.

Look at Diego Simeone at Atletico Madrid. Do you think he was appointed Atletico manager because he is the friend, brother or son of the chairman? No, he was given the position because of his ability. The president thought he was the best man for the job. He has just been rewarded with a new four year contract because of his achievements at the Vicente Calderon Stadium. I was a favourite of Freddy Shepherd's mother. Does that make me suitable to manage Newcastle? No it does not. You can say the same about Arsene Wenger, Jose Mourinho and even Alex Ferguson. Can the Newcastle hierarchy claim to have those same ambitions or interests for their club? Joe Kinnear, Denis Wise and Alan Pardew were all friends of the owner.

Mike Ashley needs to make a statement of intent, unlike his interview, prior to the 2014-15 season's nail-biting must-win clash against West Ham. He appeared to wash his hands of appointing a new manager. That responsibility lies with Lee Charnley and his football board. Without being disrespectful to Charnley, but what are his footballing credentials? Does he have any experience in football or any understanding of the game? In the past Ashley has been surrounded by his drinking buddies; people who have watched Sky Sports News or played Subbuteo and Super Striker.

You would like to think this isn't the case anymore.

Supporters still talk about when we thrashed Manchester United 5-0 and Barcelona 3-2. Those games where back in 1996 and 1997! Why can't the club give fans more of those games? I know I keep saying this but imagine what it would do to the city if Newcastle won a trophy? The Premier League may be out of reach but there is no reason they can't win the FA Cup, League Cup or the Europa League?

Nobody wants to remember the part Mike Ashley has played in United's history. It has been a calamity from day one. Wearing the club's shirts and sitting and drinking in the stands! What was all that about? He changed the name of St James' Park, for god's sake. It feels like he is on a perpetual mission to intentionally wind up Newcastle supporters.

The team that Keegan put together was fantastic. I have never had that comradeship, camaraderie and companionship anywhere in my career like I had at Newcastle. We looked forward to everything, whether it was a training session, a drink or a game. Everyone was together: the team, supporters and the city. You would walk the streets of Newcastle and it felt like you were part of this great big family.

I remember this one time my wife and I had been out for something to eat down the Quayside. It was quite late at night and the queue for the taxi was about 100 yards long and I was at the back. Then all of a sudden someone recognised me and screamed, 'Hey, it's Pav! Howay to the front, Pav.' And this guy walked my wife and I to the front of the queue and held open the door on the taxi for us and wished us good night. The people in the queue must have been waiting for ages. Yet, no one in the queue complained. Not one person had any opposition to me getting in the cab. I know when some people have a drink they change and maybe become more aggressive. It could have turned nasty; but not here. Instead they clapped and sang my name. It was incredible. Where else would this happen and where else would you get this sort of treatment?

The Czech Republic people know that I played nearly 50 times for my country and that I played a few seasons in the Czech League but they haven't a clue about my life in England or Newcastle. Maybe if they knew my story they would hold me in the same esteem as Petr Kouba and Petr Cech. I'm guessing their stories would be how many titles and trophies they won. My story isn't like that. My story is how many people I won over.

I'm not trying to be big headed or get above my station in life, far from it. But when I look back at those five years under Kevin, the adulation my colleagues and I received from Magpies' supporters has never been replicated. I reckon only the superstars at Barcelona or Real Madrid are looked upon as favourably as we were. And when you consider I was no Lionel Messi or Cristiano Ronaldo you can measure how highly we were regarded. That is why I always have time for supporters when they ask for my autograph. And that is why if someone asks me to go along to a function and present some trophies for a kids' football team I always oblige. I want to give something back to them.

I know I wasn't greatest goalkeeper that ever played for Newcastle. But I must have had something for them to take me to their hearts they way they did. I never quit, when I could've done, and I always gave my best. Maybe that is what the Geordies love about me. I have never had a big house or a big car or won any trophies but playing for Newcastle makes up for any of that.

The Geordies took me to their hearts and it means more than anyone could probably understand. That feeling of belonging is hard to explain but I certainly found my spiritual home on Tyneside.

Howay the lads!

STATS

1990-91	Banik Ostrava	30
1991-98	Newcastle United	150
1998	Banik Ostrava	6
1998-00	Sheffield Wednesday	44
2000-03	Brescia	32
2003	AS Cocenza	9
2003-04	Portsmouth	3
2004	West Ham	3
2004-06	Beira Mar	63
2006-07	Newcastle United	2
1994-2001	Czech Republic	49

ACKNOWLEDGEMENTS

To the people outside of football, teachers:
Mr Šmuk, who introduced me to sport and a very good gymnast in his own right; Miss Malá, a teacher at elementary school nobody liked, always pulled our hair, hit us with a little stick, which really hurt, but introduced discipline into my life; Mr Sobota; Mr Kuchař and Mr Bracháček, a great sportsman who helped with my studies at high school; Mrs Schneidrová, a gymnast, who taught me how to somersault and loop and Mrs Svarovská, the greatest lady teacher ever. Not forgetting my schoolmate from elementary school Radim Novotný, my best friend for life.

To the coaches:
Lojza Pavelka; Jan Kudlík; Günter Cviner; Dušan Mikšík; Jaroslav Gürtler; Jaroslav Jánoš; Milan Poštůlka; František Kuldánek; Továrek; Svoboda; Kotrla Jarda, a fantastic goalkeeper who was good to me as a 15-year-old in Bohumín; Kryvult Josef, a former weightlifter, who coached his son and I, despite not being a footballer, teaching us about strength, balance and agility; František Schmucker, who shared goalkeeping secrets when I joined Banik Ostrava; Giacomo Viollini, goalkeeper coach in Brescia and Bruno Fantini, a goalkeeper coach in Cosenza, a fantastic character. We shared many good times during our six months together living in the club's hotel;

Carlo Mazzone, head coach of Brescia, a hard but fair man; Milan Máčala, who gave me an opportunity in Banik Ostrava when I was a 17-year-old kid; John 'Budgie' Burridge, a unique person; Dušan Uhrin, who gave me my first taste of international football; Jindřich Dejmal, my coach in the Czech Army in Tábor, always fought for his soldiers; David Kreisel, my best friend at Banik Ostrava and best man at my wedding; Giuliano Sbrini, my neighbour and always a great help; my uncle Jiří Hankulič, a football fan, whose dream was to see me play for Banik Ostrava; Ivo Viktor, goalkeeper coach in the Czech Army and national team and probably the greatest goalkeeper in Czech history.

Special thanks to:
Liduska; Steve Harper, a great lad, great goalkeeper for Newcastle United; my understudy and a privilege to call a friend; Alan Shearer, a legend, who wrote the foreword to the book and helped promote it; Jim Smith, who bought me to Newcastle from Banik Ostrava; Kevin Keegan; Steve Black; Glenn Roeder for bringing me back to Newcastle and allowing me to finish my playing career at St James' Park; Jimmy Montgomery, a Sunderland legend he may be, but the greatest coach I had at Newcastle; Terry Gennoe; Lenny Hepple, Denis and Lesley Martin. Denis has been like a second father to me; Tina McAloon; Roy Hutchinson, a good friend from the first day I came to Newcastle and father and son John Dent senior and John Dent junior, who came to watch me train

everyday in Durham; Lorenzo Terrinoni, one of my best friends in Newcastle, who has an Italian restaurant, Sapori Cafe, in Sandyford, a great chef and always looks after my stomach; Tom Sweeney, another of my Geordie best friends, who works for Barbour; Paul and Jane Smith; Michael Offord, who always looked after my family; Mick Dinning, who delivered Chinese food to my house and became a good friend; Natalie Hubbard for all her help and support when I'm in Newcastle; Kev and Dave at the Back Page; Dunston UTS FC fans and committee; the Toon Army, of course; Steve Wraith, who looks after me now and hopefully for many more years to come; Stuart Wheatman, who helped publish my autobiography with Steve Wraith, and Will Scott, for writing my book. We had a lot of fun with this when Will came to see me in the Czech Republic.

Special, special thanks goes to:
My three sisters: Marie, Božena and Eliška, for their support when I was a child; my brother Milan, who helped with a difficult period of my life.

It's always difficult to remember everyone I've met and who has helped in my life and, I don't want to forget anyone so, to all those I've missed, thank you.

Pavel Srnicek

ABOUT THE AUTHOR

Will Scott is a writer and journalist. His first novel is called 'Scoop'.

ABOUT THE PUBLISHER

Like us on Facebook: Mojo Risin' Publishing

Follow us on twitter: @mojorisinbooks